The LIFE *and* TEACHING *of* JESUS CHRIST

James S Stewart

SAINT ANDREW PRESS

EDINBURGH

First published in 1933 by
THE CHURCH OF SCOTLAND COMMITTEE
ON THE RELIGIOUS INSTRUCTION OF YOUTH
Copyright © The Church of Scotland Committee
on the Religious Instruction of Youth 1933, 1957, 1965

Published in 1977 (with minor amendments) by
SAINT ANDREW PRESS
121 George Street, Edinburgh

Reprinted 1981, 1986
Reprinted (with minor revisions) 1995

Copyright © James S Stewart 1977

ISBN 0 7152 0705 9

British Library Cataloguing in Publication Data
A catalogue record for this book
is available from the British Library.

ISBN 0-7152-0705-9

Design concept by Mark Blackadder
Cover Photograph depicting 'Christ disputing with the Doctors', by
Bernardino Butinone, courtesy of the National Galleries of Scotland
Printed and bound in Great Britain by Athenæum Press Ltd, Gateshead, Tyne & Wear

Contents

I	*The Gospel records*	1
II	*The Fulness of the Time*	11
III	*Childhood and Youth*	20
IV	*The Coming of the Call*	30
V	*The Desert*	39
VI	*The Gospel of the Kingdom*	48
VII	*The First Twelve*	58
VIII	*The Teaching Method of Jesus*	68
IX	*The Fatherhood of God*	77
X	*Sin and its Remedy*	86
XI	*The Ministry of Healing*	97
XII	*The Prayer Life of Jesus*	105
XIII	*The Great Confession*	115
XIV	*The Royal Law of Love*	127
XV	*Jesus and Social Questions*	137
XVI	*The Gathering Storm*	150
XVII	*The Last Days*	162
XVIII	*Jesus on Trial*	175
XIX	*Calvary*	184
XX	*The Triumph*	195
XXI	*Master and Lord of Life*	207
	Book References	218

'To the wife of the author'
~ Original Dedication ~

I

The Gospel records

1 *The* MAKING *of the* GOSPELS

JESUS wrote no autobiography. He left nothing in writing at all. He committed himself and his teaching simply to the hearts and memories of the men who knew and loved him. And they did not fail him. The four little books that we call Gospels are our primary, and practically our only, sources of information about the life and the words that have changed the world. We may wish the story had been told with greater fulness and detail; but we know that, short as it is, it is enough. It has given Christ to every race and age.

Strictly speaking, the Gospels are not biographies at all. The earthly life of Jesus covered more than thirty years, yet you can read these little books at a sitting. Long periods of Jesus' life are passed over in complete silence. If everything were told, says John, 'the world itself could not contain the books that should be written' (John 21:25). What we have is a set of 'memoirs', selected historical reminiscences. But it is a selection with a purpose. 'These are written that ye might believe that Jesus is the Christ, the Son of God; and that, believing, ye might have life through his name' (John 20:31). Each of the Evangelists aims at giving a portrait of the Master. And each writes inevitably from his own angle. Hence we have really four distinct portraits of Jesus. That is vitally important for us today, for Jesus is ever so much bigger and more wonderful than any one individual's view of him could possibly be. But while each portrait has its own distinctive features, they are all the same Jesus, with 'the light of the knowledge of the glory of God' upon his face.

At a later time, other 'Gospels' made their appearance; but these are rightly excluded from the New Testament, for in them fact and legend were inextricably mingled. Certain 'unwritten sayings of Jesus' (*ie* sayings not recorded in the Gospels) have also come to light, but the authenticity of these is doubtful. Famous amongst them are the following: 'Let not him who seeks cease until he finds, and when he finds he shall be astonished, astonished he shall reign, and having reigned he shall rest.' 'Raise the stone, and there thou shalt find me; cleave the wood, and there am I.' 'Whoso is near me is near the fire.'

The earliest of our four Gospels appeared probably between the years 65 to 70, that is to say, some 35 to 40 years after the earthly ministry of Jesus had closed. Why was that long interval allowed to elapse? Nowadays when a great man dies, his friends would not dream of allowing a whole generation and more to pass before publishing his *Life*; were not the Evangelists unpardonably dilatory about their obvious duty?

No, it was not dilatoriness. Probably one reason for the delay was that they, and indeed all the early Church, were so busy evangelising the world, so absorbed in their active service, so convinced that the King's business required haste, that literary work of any kind was crowded out. Nor must we forget that the bulk of these early Christians were living in expectation of a speedy end to the age. (Had not Jesus himself said, 'The kingdom of heaven is at hand,' and again, 'This generation shall not pass till all these things be fulfilled'?). This was an expectation that made the writing of books a superfluity. Moreover, the continued presence of the risen, exalted Christ with his followers was so vivid and so real to many of them that they may not have felt at first the need to be continually going back to what Jesus had said and done in the days of his flesh. Hence the days grew into months, and the months into years, and a generation had gone before the first of our Gospels appeared.

No doubt fragmentary accounts of isolated sayings and deeds of Jesus were in existence before the Evangelists wrote. St Luke, for example, in the opening verses of his Gospel, tells us that he had a large quantity of such miscellaneous materials to sift out and to draw upon in constructing his own narrative. Here a parable would have been preserved in writing, there the story of a miracle, there a group of sayings, there a body of teaching on some special subject – the Sabbath, or fasting, or prayer. To that extent the Evangelists found the way prepared. These verses (Luke 1:1-4) should be carefully read and studied. They are of extreme importance for determining what Biblical 'inspiration' means, and what it does not mean. Luke there makes it perfectly clear that the inspired writers were not miraculously freed from the necessity of hard historical research which other writers have to face. Inspiration was not God magically transcending human minds and faculties: it was God expressing his will through the dedication of human minds and faculties. It does not supersede the sacred writer's own personality and make him God's machine: it reinforces his personality and makes him God's living witness.

When at last the impulse to write down the story of Jesus began to make itself powerfully felt, various motives contributed to it. For one thing, the expectation of a sudden end of the world had by this time receded, and with the lengthening of the years and the gradual passing of the men and women who had known Jesus and been eye-witnesses of his life and death and resurrection, it became obvious that to continue to rely on oral tradition and on fragmentary documents would be extremely precarious. The Evangelists felt a call to save the story of Jesus for unborn generations. Moreover, there were the needs of the thousands of young converts from paganism to be considered. A young person joining the Christian Church in the generation after Christ would naturally want to know what the Lord's Supper meant and how it had originated: obviously the most helpful thing to do would be to put into his hands some authoritative narrative of the events in the upper room on the night of Jesus' betrayal. Again, there was the danger of heresy to be combated. When divergent views on central matters of faith appeared within the Church, the question inevitably rose: What had Jesus actually said about this? What had he taught? Once again, when the Church was attacked from outwith, and false, damaging representations of the character and conduct and motives of its members were being circulated far and wide, what better defence could there be than simply to hold up before the eyes of the world the story of the Master who had pledged to serve? Along these different lines the need for preserving the sacred story in some definite and permanent form was growingly felt; and the Evangelists set to work.

2 *The* EARLIEST GOSPEL

St Mark's Gospel was the first to appear. Now there is a very ancient and reliable tradition (it comes from Papias, one of the earliest of Christian writers) which tells us that 'Mark became the interpreter of Peter', and that he 'wrote down accurately everything that he remembered' from Peter's discourses and sermons. That is of the utmost importance. It gives us a picture of young John Mark accompanying the great Apostle on his preaching tours, standing in the market-place while Peter preached to the crowds, and helping Peter to deal with inquirers when the meeting was over. We see Mark listening again and again to the story of the life and death of Jesus as it came from Peter's lips, until he knew that story by heart himself, and was living in the atmosphere of it; and when at last death claimed his great friend and leader, and Mark was left alone, he wrote the story down. And so the earliest Gospel was given to the world. It is a great thing to know that behind it stands the witness of Peter, one of the Master's most intimate friends. Hence its historical authority is beyond dispute.

The words, 'The Gospel according to St Mark', which stand in our Authorised Version at the beginning of this little book, are a later addition. Mark himself gave no name. The Evangelists were not seeking literary reputation. Their passion for the glory of Christ had submerged every thought of self. They were not concerned that the world should know from whose hands the story had come. It is in keeping with this, too, that they tell the story with the utmost frankness and candour, never seeking to present the disciple-band in a specially favourable light, or to minimise their blunderings and faults. Mark's Gospel, as we have seen, is really Peter's story. Peter has certainly not tried to save himself! 'He rebuked Peter, saying, "Get thee behind me, Satan"' (8:33); 'they all forsook him and fled' (14:50); the story of Peter's denial (14:66ff) – it is all here, with nothing hidden, nothing palliated. Earthly fame was nothing to these men: the beauty of Christ was everything.

But if Mark is silent about himself, we can gather a good deal about him from other parts of the New Testament. The following passages in Acts should be consulted: 12:12 (which provides us with the interesting suggestion that Mark's home may have been the home of 'the upper room' and the Last Supper, in which case Mark himself may well have been an eye-witness of Jesus); 12:25; 13:13; 15:36ff; also the following references in the Epistles: Colossians 4:10; II Timothy 4:11; Philemon 24; I Peter 5:13.

Mention should be made of one exceptionally attractive and fascinating suggestion, namely that within the Gospel itself at one point (Mark 14:51f) there is a veiled reference to the writer. Who was this 'certain young man' who appears so mysteriously in Gethsemane? Only Mark of the four Evangelists records the incident. Nor can Peter be his authority here: Peter had already fled (14:50). The story must have come from the 'young man' himself. And there would have been no point in recording it, unless he had been someone fairly prominent in the early Church of subsequent days. May not the nameless figure in Gethsemane have been Mark himself? It is impossible, of course, to settle the matter definitely; but at least the identification seems not improbable.

3 *The* GOSPEL *for* JEWISH CHRISTIANS

When we turn from Mark's little book of 'memoirs of Jesus' to that of Matthew, one difference strikes us immediately. Mark's principal interest is in the events of Jesus' life: Matthew concentrates rather on his teaching. Another early Christian tradition (again from Papias) tells us that 'Matthew wrote down the sayings of Jesus in Hebrew, and each interpreted these as best he could'. It seems that Matthew the disciple had a diary in which he entered from time to time the conversations and the teaching of his Master, and this diary, added to Mark's narrative, became the basis of the Gospel that now bears his name. It is specially a Gospel for Jewish Christians. Note in this connection the frequency of Old Testament quotations, the importance attached to the Mosaic law, and the emphasis on the Jewish Messianic hope and its fulfilment in Jesus.

With the modesty which, as we have already seen, characterises all the Evangelists, Matthew tells the story of his own conversion in a single verse (9:9). Nor is any effort made to conceal the depths from which Christ had lifted him: he was a tax-gatherer, 'sitting at the receipt of custom', a man, that is to say, socially ostracised, for he had sold country and conscience, and probably character as well, in a profession which, in the eyes of every loyal Jew, was branded as dishonourable. In what unlikely places Christ finds his evangelists and ambassadors!

4 *The* GOSPEL *for* GENTILE CHRISTIANS

St Luke is the one Evangelist who was not a Jew. He used both Mark and the Sayings-Source which appears in Matthew, but he had other materials as well. His Gentile birth and sympathies account for what is by far the most striking feature of his Gospel, namely that it is a *missionary* Gospel, and that the Christ it portrays is not primarily the Messiah of Israel at all, but the Saviour of the whole earth. The very fact that the book is dedicated to Theophilus – possibly a high official under the Roman Government, and not yet a Christian – is significant.

Notice, too, that at the very outset, Luke lifts the story he is going to tell out of a purely local Palestinian setting and deliberately places it in the framework of world history: not only does he trace the genealogy of Jesus right back to Adam as the founder of the race (contrast Matthew – who begins with Abraham, the founder of Israel), but he connects the coming of Jesus with world events (see, *eg* 3:1).

Moreover, the missionary motive was obviously for Luke the deciding factor in determining which particular incidents and parables, out of the mass of materials at his disposal, he should include in his published memoirs of Jesus. In this connection it is only necessary to mention the Parable of the Good Samaritan, the incident of the one grateful leper (17:11, 'and he was a Samaritan'), such sayings of Jesus as, 'They shall come from the east, and from the west, and from the north, and from the south, and shall sit down in the Kingdom of God' (13:29), and, above all, the Parable of the Prodigal Son, a story which carries a national as well as an individual reference – the younger son standing for the Gentile world and the elder son standing for the Jewish. It is pre-eminently the Gospel of a universal hope.

Luke himself, who wrote the Acts of the Apostles as well as the third Gospel (see Acts 1:1), was a physician (Colossians 4:14). It may well have been in his capacity as a doctor that Luke was first introduced to Paul, whose travelling companion he subsequently became; and we can readily understand how valuable Luke's professional skill must have been to the great Christian missionary, whose physical health was at the best precarious (II Corinthians 12:7ff), and who had frequent experience of wounds and scars and bruises in his Master's service (II Corinthians 11:25ff; Galatians 6:17; Acts 14:19).

Luke's training as a doctor also accounts for the special place given in the Gospels to the healing miracles of Jesus, and for the occurrence throughout his narrative of certain technical terms which were used in the medical language of his day. Sir William Ramsay has made the very attractive suggestion that Luke hailed originally from Philippi, though he was now resident in Asia Minor, where Paul had first met him and converted him to Christianity; and that when Paul in his dream at Troas saw 'a man of Macedonia' beckoning them to 'come over and help' (Acts 16:9), it was his friend Luke whom he saw. It would be entirely congruous with the whole spirit of the third Gospel, and with its passionate missionary interest, that its author should have been instrumental in bringing Christianity across to the Western world.

5 *The* LAST GOSPEL

When we pass from the first three Gospels (often called, because of their common viewpoint, the 'Synoptics') to the fourth, we feel at once that we are in a different atmosphere. From the earliest times this difference was felt, and the words that Clement of Alexandria quotes from a still older writer describe it well –

'John, perceiving that the bodily facts had been set forth in the other Gospels, composed a spiritual Gospel.' Clearly the author presupposes a knowledge of the other Gospels in his readers, and he sets himself to supplement their narratives, and with the aid of his own spiritual genius and mysticism to elucidate the deeper meaning of the person and work of Jesus. It was the last of the Gospels to appear, and the long thought and brooding and spiritual communion of a life-time have gone into its composition.

Among many things distinguishing this Gospel from its predecessors, the following may be mentioned. It gives us no parables. It concentrates on the Judean ministry of Jesus, to the almost entire exclusion of the ministry in Galilee. It records a whole new series of private conversations of Jesus with individuals: notably with Nathanael, with Nicodemus, with the woman of Samaria. It omits certain scenes where the human side of our Lord's nature is stressed, notably the temptation in the desert, the agony in the garden, and the cry of dereliction from the Cross. It stresses the eternal aspects of Christ's person and work. It gives us, not the Carpenter of Nazareth, but 'the Word that was in the beginning with God'.

It is not likely that the Gospel in its present form is the work of John the Apostle. Other hands have worked over it (see *eg* 19:35; 21:24). But behind it we are justified in tracing the figure of the great Apostle; and the view can be strongly supported that this wonderful Gospel, in some ways the most wonderful of them all, was built up partly from reminiscences written down by 'the disciple whom Jesus loved', perhaps in the form of a diary (cf Matthew above), shortly after the events themselves, and partly from historical sermons on the life of Jesus preached by him subsequently in Ephesus. Certainty on these matters will perhaps never be attained. What does matter is that the fourth Gospel, in setting out to supplement the other three, has gloriously achieved its purpose, and *more* than achieved it. It has made our picture of Jesus the Son of God full and perfect and complete.

So much, then, for our records. It is on these four little books that all our study of the Life and Teaching of Jesus must be based. And let us remember that they give us three things. They give us *History*. Here we have a solid bedrock of historic fact, fixed and impregnable. But they give us something more than History: they give us *Revelation*. For as we turn the pages, it is God's voice that we hear, God's face that we see. But they give us more than History and Revelation: they give us *a Challenge*. Every page renews the challenge, every line drives it home. And the challenge is – 'What *think* ye of Christ?' That first, and then – 'What shall I *do* with Christ?'

And the challenge haunts us until we answer.

II

The Fulness of the Time

1 *A* WORLD PREPARED

IN the Church of the Holy Sepulchre in Jerusalem, one spot is pointed out to travellers as being the centre of the world. It is a strange and rather fantastic claim. Yet there is a sense in which the corner of the earth's surface called Palestine is the geographical centre. Take the three great continents of Europe, Asia, and Africa: in between them, linking them up, lies this little land-bridge on the eastern shores of the Mediterranean. Clearly, if you were to start a movement whose aim was to extend out into the three great continents simultaneously, that neck of land would be a natural starting point. The old legend about the centre of the world is, therefore, truer than the men who invented it realised. It was no haphazard thing that made Bethlehem and Nazareth and Calvary the cradle of the Christian faith. It was the best possible place for the launching of a world-religion.

But if the place God chose was ideal for the coming of the Christ, the time God chose was ideal too; and it is this we are now to consider. It was when the fulness of the time was come, says Paul, that God sent forth his Son (Galatians 4:4). That is to say, it was when world conditions were exactly ripe for it that God's supreme revelation in history came. It was when all the factors – social, economic, moral, religious – had converged upon him that the Man of God's right hand came forth.

Now, God be thanked Who has matched us with His hour
And caught our youth, and wakened us from sleeping.

So sang Rupert Brooke. And never did it happen more gloriously than when Jesus came forth from the bosom of God. The hour and the Man had met.

Search the pages of history up and down, and in all the tale of the centuries you will not find any generation in which Christ could better have come than just the generation in which he did come. 'There is a tide,' says Shakespeare, 'in the affairs of men.' We can go beyond that and say that there is a tide in the affairs of God: and it is when that tide reaches the flood, when all the preparatory work is done and world conditions are clamouring for it and human souls are open, it is then, at the flood-tide hour of history, that God launches his new adventure. So it was when Luther sent his Ein' feste Burg ringing and singing along the roads of Europe. So it was when Scotland heard the rugged voice of John Knox. So it was when Wesley kindled a great fire in England. So it was supremely when upon the whole Graeco-Roman world there burst suddenly out of Galilee, with the shouts of saints and the trumpetings of angels, the sound of a new name, the name of Jesus. It was the fulness of the time, said Paul – it was the hour foreordained in the divine wisdom – when God sent forth his son. Jesus came at the very point in history at which all the conditions were ripe for his coming.

The practical value of this study of world conditions at the birth of Christ lies in the discovery that modern conditions are closely parallel. It is the growing conviction, the considered judgement of those who can read the signs of the times that once again in world relations – social, economic, moral, and religious – God's flood-tide is coming, and that our generation is seeing what people saw twenty centuries ago: the lines of preparation beginning to converge, beginning to point to a new day of the power of the Son of Man. Today, as then, God is matching the hour with the Christ, and there is an opportunity now, unprecedented for nineteen hundred years, for Christ's evangel to get a lasting grip. For Jesus and for mankind the fulness of the time draws nigh.

2 *The* POLITICAL PREPARATION

Let us look now at some of the converging lines of preparation that made things ripe for Jesus when first he came.

We begin with this. *When Jesus came, it was the fulness of the time politically.* What was the dominating feature of the political situation of the generation to which Christ came? It was the unification of the world. That was Caesar's achievement. The day of closed frontiers was over. The day of separate, self-sufficient, antagonistic nations, gazing suspiciously at one another across bristling defences, was done. All the way from the Atlantic to the Caspian, from Britain to the Nile, from Hadrian's Wall to the Euphrates, the Roman standards could be seen. Everywhere the barriers were down. The chaos had been consolidated into a community. The world was one big neighbourhood.

Three factors contributed to this situation into which the Gospel of Christ was born. One was *the Roman Peace*. If Christ had come a century earlier, his Gospel would have been blocked at every turn: blocked on the land by closed national frontiers, blocked on the ocean by the pirates who made the high seas impassible. Or if he had come a few centuries later, he would have found civilisation too pre-occupied with its terrible struggle against the barbarian hordes from the north to have any ear for the Gospel. But Christ came to a generation when the Roman Peace held the world, held it no doubt with an iron hand, but held it sure and far-flung and unbroken; and men could hear the Bethlehem angels sing.

A second factor making for the unity of the world when Jesus came was *the great Roads*. From end to end of the Empire the great highways ran, triumphs of Roman engineering. And the 10,000 labourers who had toiled on the making of the roads, in the sweat of their brows, little thought they were preparing a way for the Son of God. But they were. Along these Imperial lines of communication, built to carry Caesar's legions to every corner of his dominions, the missionaries of the Gospel came marching; and everywhere their message spread like wild-fire. Christ's men could never have evangelised the world as they did if it had not been for the Roman Roads.

The third factor making for world unity when Jesus came was *Language*. Imagine what would have happened if the first missionaries had barriers of language to contend with. Their advance would have been slowed down, and terribly retarded, in many places brought to a standstill, and that at a stage in their great adventure when it was absolutely vital to lose no time. But as it was, wherever they went, they found there was one language that carried them through. For while each province still had its own tongue or dialect, everywhere the people were bilingual and all knew Greek. In the heights of Galatia as much as on the streets of Athens, in Spain as in Rome, the missionaries could speak Greek knowing that they would be understood.

The Roman Peace, the great Roads, the common Language – these were the things that had linked the world up into one big neighbourhood, and so had prepared the way for Christ.

Compare the present day. Is history not repeating itself? The big fact that is revolutionising the life of all the peoples of the earth today is this: that the world in more recent times has shrunk amazingly, that the ends of the earth have been brought far closer together than ever they were before, that our contacts with our fellow men have been multiplied almost bewilderingly. Nothing of importance can happen in any corner of the world without being known and discussed by people on the other side of the world in a matter of hours, even minutes. And the great thing about the new contacts is that they are not merely physical and mechanical contacts: they are moral and spiritual. Start a new idea in Britain or in Russia or in India, and before long the new idea has put a girdle round the earth. It is not only words that fly faster and farther today than ever before: the thoughts of people's hearts are doing it too.

What a chance for Jesus, and what a responsibility for the Church of Jesus! Only let one nation, one Church, one congregation, one soul begin to burn for Christ, and in less time than it takes to tell, the heather might be on fire for Christ across *all* the earth. Only let one little body of Christ's people anywhere, here in our own land, if God will, feel the urgency of a new Pentecost, the inward power of the Lord Jesus, and it might not be long until on the other side of the world they were taking the Kingdom of Heaven by storm. 'Behold, I have set before thee an open door' (Revelation 3:8). In God's grace it is wide open today, and the fulness of the time is nigh.

3 *The* ECONOMIC PREPARATION

When Jesus first came, it was the fulness of the time, not only politically, but also economically. Deep down beneath the shining culture of that old world, down beneath its luxury and magnificence, unrest was seething and poverty walked in rags. Two out of every three on the streets of Rome were slaves, mere goods and chattels; and sometimes the slave heart rebelled. And when the great poets of Rome sang of the Golden Age, it was generally to the past that they turned their eyes. Not for them, as for the Hebrew prophets, did the Age of Gold lie in front, shining in a happy, beckoning future; the Golden Age of plenty lay behind them, and it was the Age of Iron now.

Indeed, in many of Caesar's dominions, the economic situation had reached the point of crisis when Jesus came. So it was in Palestine. The disastrous aftermath of war, the wild colossal extravagance of Herod the Great, the burden of taxation, both civil and religious, the growing over-population which made it impossible for the land to provide food enough for its own inhabitants – these things had precipitated a period of un-exampled depression among the great bulk of the people. Life had grown care-ridden and full of worry. Anxiety for the mor-row was written deep upon people's faces and on their hearts; and all the world seemed tangled and gone wrong. It was then, at the blackest hour, that a Voice of hope rang out in Galilee; and people's hearts leapt up and listened, for the fulness of the time had come.

Here is a question worth discussion. Do revivals of religion come more easily in times of economic prosperity or in times of economic depression? No doubt many may grow so desperately worried and care-ridden about material things, about the question of where tomorrow's bread is going to come from, that they may have little or no heart or interest left for religion. But no doubt, also, our extremity is still God's opportunity; and the very breakdown of all human resources may prepare the world at last to listen to Christ. Certainly it has been out of some of the most depressed and desperate human situations that the great historic revivals have burst, like the break of a new day. And who can say but that all our own distresses have been preparing for a new coming of the living Christ into human history, and making straight through the desert a highway for our God? Economically, no less than politically, the fulness of the time has come.

4 *The* MORAL PREPARATION

When Jesus first came, it was the fulness of the time morally. Swinburne, in one of his poems, cries out protestingly that after Christ the world has never known the same light-heartedness again; that Jesus has taken all its natural gaiety and good spirits away; that until then the Graeco-Roman world had been perfectly happy and innocent and contented in its Nature-worship, its worship of Zeus and Dionysus and Aphrodite; that Jesus really spoilt everything.

Thou hast conquer'd, O pale Galilean;
the world has grown grey from thy breath.

But all that is false to the facts. Historically, it is nonsense. The idea of an ancient world happy and innocent and light-hearted and morally at peace is simply a myth. If you want the real truth about that world you will get it, not in Swinburne, but in St Paul, in that terrible picture that stands for ever for all future ages to read in Paul's first chapter to the Romans – a world that was sunk in moral hopelessness. 'The world was growing old,' says Mommsen. 'Not even Caesar could make it young again.' No, indeed, for it had sinned its youth away, and all the freshness of the dew of youth was gone, and only the worm, the canker, and the grief were left. Everywhere the best spirits were in despair. Everywhere to the noblest souls it seemed that the whole world was pursuing its riotous way down to disaster and oblivion and ultimate night. And it was then Christ came, travelling in the greatness of his strength, and made the old world new.

May we not say that some such impact of the Spirit of Christ upon the moral life of mankind and nations is one of the prime needs of today? When the experiment of slackening morality and tampering with codes of honour has been carried to a certain point, inevitably there comes a reaction. Inevitably that something of God which lurks beneath the surface of our hearts stands up and records its protest. The glamour of the sensationalist creed and the lure of the modern gospel of uncontrol have the living Christ to reckon with. Mankind will not be satisfied with the ethics of the dust always. They are increasingly rebellious against them now. In the moral sphere, the fulness of the time has come.

5 *The* RELIGIOUS PREPARATION

When Jesus first came, it was in the fulness of the time religiously. The old gods of Rome were either dead or dying. To fill the gap, two expedients were tried. On the one hand, a whole new batch of gods was imported from the East: outlandish, Oriental deities brought in to stir Rome's jaded senses – till amongst the philosophers the overcrowding of Olympus, where the gods were supposed to dwell, became a standing joke. On the other hand, the strange phenomenon of Caesar-worship appeared: the Emperor himself was accorded divine honours. But all expedients failed. What was a whole Pantheon of gods worth if they had nothing to say to a man or woman with a broken heart? What could the divinity of Caesar say to a soul stabbed with the remorse of sin? When everything had been done that could be done, the hungry hearts of people were hungry still.

But there was something more definite than that. There was a strange sense of something impending from the side of God. In many parts of the world, men of deeper nature and more spiritual vision were peering into the darkness for some faint flush of dawn. Amongst the Jews themselves the hope of the Messiah was blazing more clearly than it had done for centuries. The great mass of Jewish literature from the period between the Old Testament and the New Testament is full of this great hope. And when any new voice rang out across the land – the voice of John the Baptist, for instance – immediately on every lip there rose the question: 'Is this the Messiah now?'

The air was tense with expectation. And the Jews, penetrating as they did into every corner of the Empire, took that great dream with them and handed it on. Nothing cleared the way for Christ more definitely than that passionate hope. The fulness of the time had come.

Today, in the religious sphere, the same spirit is at work. On the one hand, just as in the Roman Empire, the old gods are dead or dying. The gods of convention, the gods of out-worn, second-hand religious tradition, the gods of materialism and secularism are losing grip. And on the other hand, our generation is marked by a sudden new outbreak of interest in Jesus. Witness the books about Christ that recent years have produced. Witness the fact that outside Christendom altogether – in India, for example – people are looking to Jesus of Nazareth for guidance. Witness the new spiritual awakening amongst youth. Witness a score of similar significant facts. One thing is certain: where Jesus is concerned today, the spiritual tide is rising. And it may be that our very generation is going to see the flood coming in across the ramparts of the Church and of the world irresistibly. The fulness of time is nigh.

So the Redeemer came. Somewhere in the mind and heart of God, from the very foundation of the earth, the Christ had been waiting, hidden in the counsels of eternity until the great bell of the ages should strike; and when at last everything in the world and in the souls of mankind was ready and prepared, he came, the Word of God made flesh, not a moment early and not a moment late, but exactly on the stroke of the hour. It was the Day of the Lord.

It is still the Day of the Lord, whenever another soul enthrones him.

'Even so, come, Lord Jesus.'

III

Childhood and Youth

1   *The* WORLD'S WELCOME *to its* REDEEMER

IT was the fulness of the time. And yet on the day when Christ entered it, the world looked inhospitable enough. 'There was no room for him in the inn' (Luke 2:7). The innkeeper's refusal to the weary travellers that night was a foretaste of what was coming.

Why did the innkeeper refuse? He refused partly, no doubt, because he was too busy. The census of Caesar Augustus was a good thing in its way, he told himself, for it filled his house with guests and his pockets with money; but being an innkeeper in census time was no sinecure, and from early morning till far into the night the jostling crowds had kept him busy, and certainly he had no time to waste listening to two belated travellers with a strange story of distress. He refused, also, because to have welcomed Joseph and Mary would have meant turning two of his other guests out. Not under any circumstances, he told himself, could he do that. Probably he refused, also, because he saw that the man and woman standing outside in the cold night were poor and shabby. If Joseph and Mary had been able to hold up a purse of gold, would there still have been no room? We wonder. At any rate, it is worth noticing that the same motives *still* operate to close the door on Christ. People are too busy; or they know that if Christ came in, certain other things would have to go; or they have set their hearts on something different from one who was poor and lowly and despised and rejected, whose symbol was a Cross. 'He came unto his own, and his own received him not' (John 1:11).

Yet even so, Christ was not quite unwelcomed. The Evangelists record four deeply significant welcomes.

(1) *The Evangelists record the welcome of his mother.* Scripture is continually exalting motherhood. In the Decalogue (Exodus 20:12); in the description of the ideal mother in Proverbs, whose children 'arise up and call her blessed' (Proverbs 31:28); in the sublime passage where God himself takes a mother's love as the nearest thing to his own (Isaiah 66:13); and in the noble line of mothers that the portrait-gallery of the Old and New Testaments presents (Hannah, and Ruth and the lady of Shunem, and Elizabeth, and Salome, and Eunice, and many more) – motherhood is acclaimed and exalted.

But in lonely and unapproachable honour stands Mary, the mother of Jesus. From these pages there shines out *her devoutness.* Out of all the women in the world, God chose her to make the home in which the world's Redeemer should be reared. It was at Mary's knee that Jesus lisped his first childhood prayers.

There shines out also *her loneliness.* She was lonely in the sublime destiny for which God appointed her, lonely in the deep thoughts she kept and pondered in her heart (Luke 2:19), lonely on the morning when Jesus left his boyhood home and turned his face to the world, loneliest of all on the day when 'there stood by the cross of Jesus his mother' (John 19:25). There shines out also *her glad self-sacrifice:* 'Be it unto me according to thy word,' she said to God (Luke 1:38); and even when the sword of which Simeon spoke was piercing her (Luke 2:35), her spirit could still exult in the beauty and strength and holiness of the son whom God had given her.

(2) *The Evangelists record the welcome of the shepherds.* The story of their presence at the cradle was peculiarly appropriate. In ancient Israel, the figure of the shepherd was always closely

connected with God, as in that greatest of Israelite songs, 'The Lord is my Shepherd' (Psalm 23). Moreover, the Son of God was to be a shepherd himself, the Good Shepherd, giving his life for the sheep (John 10:11). And is there not a world of meaning in the fact that it was very ordinary people, busy about their very ordinary tasks, whose eyes first saw 'the glory of the coming of the Lord'? It means, first, that the place of duty, however humble, is the place of vision. And it means, second, that it is the men who have kept to the deep, simple pieties of life, and have not lost the child-heart, to whom the gates of the Kingdom most readily open.

Other illustrations of this could be given. To Simon Peter, the vision came out in a boat on the lake in the dawn (Luke 5:8). To Brother Lawrence, it came as he trudged a country road one day and saw a bare, wintry tree putting forth the first buds of spring. To Joan of Arc, it came in the village church of her girlhood. To Francis Thompson, it came in the roar of London's streets: Jacob's ladder – so he said – was 'pitched betwixt Heaven and Charing Cross'.

(3) *The Evangelists record the welcome of the Wise Men.* Tradition has it that one of these Magi was an African, while the others were Asiatics from Mesopotamia. Their presence at Bethlehem symbolised three things. It symbolised the Gospel's *challenge to adventure.* They had left their far homes for Christ, going out, like Abraham, 'not knowing whither they went'. It symbolised the Gospel's *challenge to thought.* The Magi were the trained investigators, the scientific men of their day, the thinkers. It symbolised the Gospel's *challenge to all the nations of the earth.* Out of the dim East, out of darkest Africa they came (as indeed Israel's singers of old had prophesied: *eg* 'The daughter of Tyre shall be there with a gift,' Psalm 45:12; and 'Ethiopia shall stretch out her hands unto God,' Psalm 68:31) to lay their national tributes at Jesus' feet.

Thus the Magi represent a three-fold challenge of Christianity today. Christ calls for adventurers, especially amongst the Church's youth. Christ calls for thinkers, those who will undertake that most urgent task in our generation, the baptising of the new knowledge into his name. Christ calls for the tribute of the nations, the wealth of character and loyalty and spiritual understanding that an Aggrey, a Schweitzer, a Kagawa can bring into his Kingdom.

(4) *The Evangelists record the welcome of Simeon and Anna.* It was the Simeons of that day – 'just and devout, waiting for the consolation of Israel' (Luke 2:25) – who had really saved religion for their land. Not that Palestine was irreligious. It was, indeed, almost too religious. There were the Pharisees. The Pharisees had *externalised* religion: they had made it a matter of outward observance, not of the heart. There were the Scribes. The Scribes had *professionalised* religion: they were dry ecclesiastics, not saints with the fire of God in them. There were the Sadducees. The Sadducees had *secularised* religion: they were sceptical and worldly. There were the Zealots. The Zealots had *nationalised* religion, making it a mere adjunct and slave to their one consuming ambition: 'Down with Rome and up with Jewry!'

But it was not any official party that had kept the soul of Israel alive. The real saviours of Israel were humble, obscure, devout people, who could not have argued with a scribe or a Sadducee for five minutes, and certainly would not have tried; who could have been made to look foolish by any clever Rabbi, and could not have held a candle to any fiery, loud-voiced, sabre-rattling Zealot. And yet, when it came to the really deep things of life – things like prayer, and the purity of heart that sees God – the Simeons were a thousand miles beyond all these others. It was Simeon and his like who were the leaven of the land. It was obscure, godly homes like his that were the backbone of Israel.

When Mary brought her child to the Temple, Simeon took him up in his arms and blessed him. Others never even turned

their heads to look as the peasant woman and her infant passed:
but Simeon knew. There is a moral and spiritual qualification for
recognising Jesus and for seeing God, and Simeon had it. Notice,
too, that Simeon with the child Jesus in his arms is a picture of
the old welcoming the new. If at his time of life he had been
content to dwell mainly or altogether in the past, we could
have understood it. But no – his mind was open, and eagerly
receptive, and sure that God's best was still to come. So he took
the child – symbol of the new age – and embraced him in his
arms. And then, like a weary toiler hearing the curfew ringing
through the gloaming, or like a sentry glad to be relieved at
daybreak, he spoke his *Nunc Dimittis* – 'Lord, now lettest thou
thy servant depart in peace, for mine eyes have seen thy salvation' (Luke 2:29f).

So God was incarnate. So through the coming of a little
child, the divine work of mending a broken world was begun.
'And the child grew, and waxed strong in spirit, filled with
wisdom; and the grace of God was upon him' (Luke 2:40).

2 HIS FATHER'S BUSINESS

An almost impenetrable veil hangs over the thirty years during
which the world's Redeemer was preparing for his work. Legends
in plenty about the childhood years of Jesus are recorded by
the Apocryphal writers, but these need not concern us. One
incident alone shines out like a star in the darkness of the
unrecorded years. When he reached the age of twelve, Jesus,
like other Jewish boys, became a 'Son of the Law' and could
attend the religious festivals (Luke 2:42ff).

What his feelings must have been on his first sight of the
Holy City and its Temple we can only guess. In the Temple he
was found when the festival was over. 'How is it that ye sought
me?' he asked. 'Wist ye not that I must be about my Father's

business?' (Luke 2:49) These are the first words from Jesus' lips that any Evangelist records. And they sum up his whole life. Everything in the story, right up to the crucifixion, illustrates and proves them. But Joseph and Mary at the time could not understand. Here we have the first hint of that loneliness that was to become so heavy a part of the cross that God's Christ carried (cf Luke 4:23f; John 6:66; 7:5).

The Revised Standard Version has made a noteworthy alteration in the translation of this verse. 'Wist ye not that I must be *in my Father's House?*' The Greek text allows either rendering. Whichever we adopt, the one great fact that emerges is Jesus' amazing awareness of God as Father. Amazing, yes; yet in some degree every young life, especially during its adolescent years, may come awake to that same great discovery. Adolescence is God's best chance with the soul.

After this first visit to Jerusalem, the veil falls again and hides another 18 years. How glad we should have been if the hand of one of the Evangelists had drawn back the veil a little! That more could have been revealed there seems no reason to doubt. Contemporaries of Jesus' boyhood and young manhood in Nazareth could have supplied additional material. Moreover, it is possible that amongst the sources on which St Luke drew for the compilation of his Gospel was Mary herself; if so, the Evangelist's knowledge of the silent years must have been considerable. But none of our records has chosen to let us into the secret. Perhaps it is better so. The hand that has drawn the veil is the hand of reverence. The silent years of the Redeemer's preparation are holy ground.

3 BOYHOOD INFLUENCES

Certain factors, however, which entered into Jesus' preparation for his life-work can be clearly enough discerned. Here we shall mention external factors only: underneath them all lay his deep, constant, secret life of communion with God his Father.

(1) To begin with, there was *Nature.* The Gospels themselves, steeped in Nature-love, are evidence of that. Behind these pictures that have become the possession of Christendom and the spiritual teachers of the world – the lilies decked in glory (Matthew 6:28f), the golden miracle of harvest (John 4:35), the mystery of unfolding buds (Mark 4:28), the nesting of the birds (Matthew 8:20), the folding of the sheep (Luke 15:4f), and many others – there lie the observation and the zest of one who was a greater Nature-lover than any poet. Jesus was a country-bred boy, and on almost every page of the Gospels there is something reminiscent of the youthful Nazareth years when the sights and sounds of Nature 'haunted him like a passion'.

It is interesting to contrast St Paul in this respect. Paul was city-bred, and his illustrations, unlike those of Jesus, are drawn almost entirely from crowded places. Builders at work in the streets (I Corinthians 3:10ff), the sights and sounds of the military barracks (Ephesians 6:13ff), the thronged arena of the Greek games (I Corinthians 9:24ff) – these, rather than country scenes, are Paul's chosen metaphors. But the Gospel pages are scented with winds that have blown across hills and valleys and fields of springing corn; and God's care and mercy are over all.

(2) But if Nature was one factor influencing the preparation of the silent years, *Human Nature* was another. Here again the Gospels are our witness. The children playing in the market-place, and sometimes growing sulky in their play (Matthew 11:16f); the woman pestering the local magistrate until by sheer doggedness she gains her point (Luke 18:1ff); the country lad going away to see life in the great city and coming back broken and penniless and ashamed (Luke 15:11ff); the professional religionist parading his piety before a gaping group of idlers at the corner of the village street (Matthew 6:5) – these and many other pictures reveal the student of human nature. The

silent Nazareth years must have been full of that study. 'He knew all men, and required no evidence from anyone about human nature; well did he know what was in human nature' (John 2:25, Moffatt). But Jesus was much more than a student of his fellow-men. He was a lover of mankind. Through all the tragedy and comedy of life, through all their human foibles and bignesses of soul, through sin and the pitiful consequences of sin, he loved them as only God could love.

(3) A third factor was *Scripture*. Jesus' Bible was the Old Testament. This was the foundation stone of all Jewish education; and from early childhood Jesus, like all Jewish children, would be brought up in the atmosphere of Genesis and Deuteronomy and the Psalms and Isaiah and Jeremiah. Long hours of his growing manhood must have been given to poring over the sacred page. And he studied it to some purpose. When the Tempter came to him in the desert, it was with a quotation from the Old Testament that each of the three temptations was rebutted (Matthew 4:4, 7, 10). In the great prophetic picture of the invasion of human life by the divine Spirit (Isaiah 61:1ff) he saw his own work foreshadowed (Luke 4:18ff). And how powerfully the thought of the Suffering Servant (Isaiah 53) influenced his own conception of the Messianic vocation, we can realise again and again throughout the Gospel story. His soul was steeped in the great old Scriptures of his people.

Hebrew, which had ceased to be the spoken tongue, was the mother-tongue of Judaism; and though the Scriptures had been translated into Greek (in the Septuagint), it was in Hebrew that Jesus read and studied them. In the common speech of the day, Hebrew had given place to Aramaic, a derivative of the same Semitic family. But with the coming of Greek, Palestine had become bilingual. No doubt, while able to use Greek at will, Jesus would familiarly think and speak in the Aramaic of the vernacular. Our Gospels, written in Greek, have preserved (possibly because of the emotion of the circumstances in which they were originally spoken) certain Aramaic expressions of our Lord's – 'Talitha cumi' (Mark 5:41), 'Ephphatha' (Mark 7:34), and 'Eloi, Eloi, lama sabachthani' (Mark 15:34). But his Old Testament quotations make it clear that he had studied his Bible in the original Hebrew.

(4) A fourth factor in the unrecorded preparatory years was *the workshop.* Jesus was Carpenter of Nazareth. It is impossible to exhaust the significance of the fact that, for a great part of his life on earth, the Son of God toiled with his hands, doing a joiner's work. 'A workshop,' said Henry Drummond, 'is not a place for making engines, so much as a place for making men.' A workshop helped to make the soul of Christ. The devoted skill and labour that went into those Nazareth yokes and ploughs and cottage tables were rendered as an offering to God. Even then Jesus was 'about his Father's business'. Hence toil has been hallowed for ever. The distinction between secular and sacred avocations vanishes. Hard work – whether manual labour or the duty of the businessman – *is* sacred when it is done as under the eyes of God.

Very dear the Cross of shame,
Where He took the sinner's blame …
But He walked the same high road,
And He bore the self-same load
When the Carpenter of Nazareth
Made common things for God.

There is a legend that, over the doors of the Carpenter's shop, there was the sign – 'my yokes are easy' (cf Matthew 11:30). Whether the sign was there or not, we can well believe that every yoke made in the shop in Nazareth was light and easy and well-fitting. Made by the same hands, the yoke for the oxen at the plough and the yokes for the disciples of the Kingdom were alike in that.

(5) Finally, there was *the home.* It must never be forgotten that Jesus was brought up in the heart of a big family (Matthew 13:55ff; Mark 6:3). Joseph seems to have died comparatively early, for his name disappears from the narrative altogether; and no doubt when Jesus grew to manhood it was upon him, as the eldest brother, that the main responsibility for the support of the home devolved. Sidelights upon the early home-life of the Master may be found in many of the parables. The turning-out of the house to find a coin that has rolled away into a dark corner and disappeared (Luke 15:8ff); the measuring of the flour and the leaven for the weekly baking (Matthew 13:33); the plight of the householder who, finding his larder empty on the arrival of an untimely guest, knocks up his churlish neighbour at midnight (Luke 11:5ff); the lighting of the candles at the gloaming hour (Matthew 5:15); the healthy appetites of children home from school and play (Matthew 7:9f) – these touches and many others are surely reminiscent of Mary's home, a home from which, in days when trade was bad, poverty could not be very far away. Certainly there was no affluence about it. 'Is not this the carpenter's son?' they said later: there was no mistaking the sneer (Matthew 13:55). But to Jesus it was home, and love was there, and God was there; and by his own devotion to it all those hidden, waiting years, he has hallowed home-life forever.

Such were the factors that entered into our Lord's preparation for his life-work. Thirty long years passed and no sign was given. There was a broken world to be mended, a lost humanity to be redeemed, and still there was no sign. Then, quite suddenly, God's hour struck; and the Son of Man came forth.

IV
The Coming of the Call

1 A VOICE *in the* WILDERNESS

THERE is always something strangely moving and fascinating in the sight of a young soul launching out into the deep and entering upon its life-work. The day when God calls you to do something – whether that call be to run a business, or to teach a school, or to work in an office, or to preach the Gospel – is one of life's great crucial days. Here we have the story of the most momentous call in history – the call of Jesus to his work of saving the world.

On one point all four Gospels are agreed: Christ's call was in some way connected with John the Baptist's preaching and with the whirlwind revival which that preaching had started. Our first step, then, is to look at this man of the desert and try to probe his secret and his power.

If you had asked any of the people in the crowds that flocked out to the Jordan to hear him what that secret and that power were, they would almost certainly have fixed on three things: this John was a man, he was a man of God, and he was a man with a message.

He was a man. He radiated vitality and virility. Even the way he lived made them feel that. For out there in the desert he had dispensed with all the mere accessories of life, clothed himself in the roughest, simplest clothing as a protest against the overdone purples and soft raiments of so many who called themselves religious, and lived on locusts and wild honey, subsisting on the bare minimum in order to prove that a man's life consisteth not in the abundance of the things which he possesseth (Luke 12:15). The very way he lived convinced the world that this was a man indeed.

Moreover, they knew him for a man by his attitude to the whole question of popularity. The very last thing John resembled was a 'reed shaken in the wind' (Matthew 11:7). Human applause and approbation meant simply nothing to him. Smooth, conventional inanities his soul hated. If a thing was true, then out with it – though they should turn and rend him for it. Pericles, the great Greek (so we are told by Plutarch), never spoke without leaving a secret sting in the hearts of his hearers. That was the Baptist's way.

You see it in his attitude to the Pharisees and Sadducees, the great men of the land. 'O generation of vipers, who hath warned you to flee?' (Matthew 3:7). You see it still better in his attitude to Herod. Herod first patronised him, applauded him, showered marks of favour on him; and Herod, remember, was a king, and it is surely something big for a desert prophet to be taken up and courted by a king. Surely the prophet will be careful in his speech, more apologetic, more ready to turn a blind eye to certain ways and practices. Will he indeed? Herod might be a king, but there was a King above kings; and if the royal law of Heaven were broken, then straight into Herod's presence John would go with flashing eyes and pointing finger and blunt rebuke: 'It is not lawful for thee!' (Matthew 14:4). Here was a real man. F W H Myers' splendid lines are true:

John, than which man a grander or a greater
Not till this day has been of woman born,
John like some iron peak by the Creator
Fired with the red glow of the rushing morn.

But he was more than a man, he was *a man of God*. That, too, drew the crowds flocking out to the desert. Here, for the first time in their lives, they had come upon a religion utterly and absolutely real, a religion real in every flaming syllable of it, real in every burning word. 'To teach religion,' said Thomas Carlyle, 'the first thing needful and the last, and indeed the only thing, is to find a man who *has* religion.' Here was a man who had religion, whose whole life and attitude breathed God!

Now that was something new. These people had been in the habit of taking their religion from the scribes, and with the scribes it was all a mass of learned subtleties and intricate sophistries, a poor, discredited, second-hand affair. But here was this new voice, blowing all that to the winds, and going right to the heart of things, like Amos seven hundred years before – 'The lion hath roared, who will not fear? The Lord God hath spoken, who can but prophesy?' (Amos 3:8). John, like Amos, came with a ringing 'Thus saith the Lord!' That was what won these people, that here at last – surprisingly and overwhelmingly – was religion utterly real. A man of God indeed!

He was a man, and a man of God. He was also *a man with a message*. Indeed, so absorbed was he in the message he had received from God for men that he forgot all about himself; his own personality was lost, swallowed up in the truth he was charged to deliver. For when the priests and Levites were sent out to investigate, and asked him who he was, his answer was – 'I am the voice of one crying in the wilderness, Make straight the way of the Lord', a voice, and nothing more. The man was nothing, the message everything. And what was the message? Nothing gentle or soft or soothing; but this, with a terrible urgency behind it, and a passionate pleading in every note of it – 'Repent! Flee from the wrath to come!'

Also of John a calling and a crying
  Rang in Bethabara, till strength was spent,
Cared not for counsel, stayed not for replying,
  John had one message for the world, 'Repent'.

2 *The* REVIVAL

Now let us turn from the preacher to his crowd. He did not have to go in search of an audience. They came in spite of themselves. And a motley audience it was. Soldiers were there, and publicans, poor folk and saddened sinners, rubbing shoulders with proud, self-satisfied Pharisees and sceptical Sadducees. The very audience proves that it was no man-made thing, this revival, but the power of the everlasting God.

What were the motives that drew them? *Some no doubt came from curiosity.* There were Jerusalem circles where it was the fashion to be able to say you had been out in the desert hearing John; and there were people there, no less than at Athens, who lived for any new thing that was happening. It is worthwhile remarking that in religion the motive of curiosity still operates. There are people who, if a revival started, would be right in the thick of it – not so much for any definitely spiritual reason, but for the new sensation. However, that motive of curiosity is not to be sneered at: many a soul who came to look (like Zacchaeus) has stayed to pray.

Others again flocked out to John *for political reasons.* For two hundred years the voice of prophecy had been silent in Israel, and now down by the Jordan it had burst out again. What could that mean but this: that a new nationalist movement was on the way, and that the heel of the oppressor was to be shaken from Israel's throat? 'Down with Rome and up with Jewry!' was the cry.

But there was a better motive than either curiosity or nationalism: there were people in that crowd who were there *because they had sins to confess.* These were the people the Baptist wanted. Every day, when his fiery preaching was over, they stayed behind for private talks; and one by one he dealt with them, helping them to make a clean breast of all life's guilty secrets, and carrying them right out into the feeling of release and liberation that making a clean breast of one understanding heart always gives. Then he took them down to the water, and baptised them for the new life. And soon his converts were scattering the glory of it across the land.

3   JESUS *and* JOHN

By and by the news of the revival reached Galilee. It reached the streets and cottages of Nazareth. It reached a humble workshop where a young carpenter was toiling at his bench. And Jesus knew that God's hour had struck, and that day he rose and went.

But what was Jesus' attitude to John, and John's revival, to be? Clearly there were three possible attitudes.

(1) For one thing, Jesus might easily have stood aloof. He might have told himself that this was a baptism of confession and repentance, and he had nothing to confess or to repent. For these others, it was all very well, a God-sent blessing for them in their sins – but it could not be for him.

(2) Again, he might have challenged and criticised it. John's gospel was so obviously imperfect, just a half-gospel indeed: ought Christ to countenance it? There were two defects in it which Christ saw.

On the one hand, it was so terribly negative. John's followers, as Jesus himself said at a later day, were like children in the market-place playing at funerals, whereas mine want to dance! The very fact that John was a desert man, an ascetic, told against him, and proved that he had somehow missed the rapturous, radiant, happy-hearted view of God for which Christ stood. 'I'll think more of your prayers,' wrote the author Robert Louis Stevenson to his father, 'when I see more of your praises!' That was where John came short, with his 'Thou shalt not' religion.

Moreover, here, saw Jesus, was a religion built on fear. 'Flee from the wrath to come.' Is fear a fit weapon for driving mankind into salvation? Here was John preaching a flaming God, and here was Christ with his heart throbbing with the news of a Father God. Ought Christ to countenance John? He might have opposed him. Andrew Bonar and Robert Murray McCheyne were walking together one day. 'McCheyne asked me,' says Bonar, 'what my last Sabbath's subject had been. It had been: "The wicked shall be turned into hell." On hearing this awful text, he asked: "Were you able to preach it with tenderness?"' There was too little tenderness about the Baptist's preaching, too much flame and denunciation: and Jesus, with his tender, loving heart, might have refused to identify himself with it in any way.

(3) But there was a third possible attitude, and it was this that Jesus took. He did not oppose, nor did he stand aloof; but in the terrific humility of God's only son, he went to John. 'Sir, I would fain be baptised of thee!'

Probably it was late at evening it happened, when the day's crowds had dispersed, and the Baptist, weary and spent, was left alone in prayer. Through the gloaming came a solitary figure, bronzed and young and clean and godlike. And when the Baptist, rising from his knees, met him, and looked into his face, and saw shining out from the eyes of him a light he had never seen before – very God of very God – and when he heard that request, 'I would be baptised of thee', suddenly the incongruity of it overwhelmed him. 'I have need to be baptised of thee, and comest thou to me?' But the quiet voice answered – 'Suffer

it to be so now: for thus it becometh us to fulfil all righteousness.' And with that, they went down into the water together
and there happened the event which the very angels might
desire to look into – a man baptising his Lord.

4 *The* INNER MEANING
of the BAPTISM *of* JESUS

How are we to interpret this mystery – the sinless Jesus under-
going a baptism meant for sinners?

Sometimes the view has been expressed that, as this was a
baptism of repentance, Jesus must have felt that he himself,
like all his brothers on the earth, had something to repent of.
Would he have sought a baptism for the remission of sins, if he
had not been conscious of sin? This we can safely reject without
more ado.

It seems likely that Jesus was moved to act as he did partly,
at least, because *he felt a real debt to John*. Here was a nation-
wide movement of revival. Spiritual issues, which for long years
had been suffering from neglect, had suddenly leapt into the
foreground. Young people and old had begun to take religion
seriously. People were worrying about their sins. They were
hungry for spiritual guidance. They were crying for the light of
God. Now obviously all this gave Jesus an enormously hopeful
atmosphere in which to begin his work. Defective as the message of the Baptist's mission was at certain points, it was nevertheless a wonderful preparation for the Gospel. John was a true
forerunner. And we may well believe that when Jesus offered
himself for baptism, he did it partly, at least, from a sense of the
debt he owed to his great predecessor, and from a recognition
that this revival which had been sweeping the land was a real
movement of the Spirit of God.

But there was another motive which must be taken into

account. Jesus went down into the Jordan *to take his stand by the side of sinners.* When you see the sinless Christ going to the sinners' baptism, you are seeing love going to a great redeeming act of self-identification. It was a prophecy of what the coming years were to bring, when the Lord of glory was to earn the name 'Friend of publicans and sinners', to go where need called, reckless of his reputation, to sit often at outcasts' tables, and to die at last between two thieves. 'He was numbered with the transgressors' (Isaiah 53:12). True, but he numbered himself with them first of all. At the Jordan, Jesus took his stand by the side of sinners, making their shame his shame, their trouble his trouble, their penitence his penitence, their burden his burden. It was the beginning of the work that was crowned at Calvary, when he carried the burden away for ever.

Hence the baptism of Jesus points to the fact that the only love which can ever possess redeeming power is a love that goes all the way and identifies itself with others. So Moses, in the day of his people's sin, stood and cried – 'Blot *me*, I pray thee, out of thy book of life which thou hast written' (Exodus 32:32). So St Paul, lamenting the blindness of his nation, exclaimed – 'I could wish that myself were accursed from Christ for my brethren, my kinsmen according to the flesh' (Romans 9:3). George Fox prayed 'to be baptised [note the word] into a sense of all conditions, that I might know the needs and feel the sorrows of all'. Father Damien's self-identification meant literal leprosy. 'Whenever I preach to my people,' he said, 'I do not say, "my brethren", as you do, but "we lepers". People pity me and think me unfortunate, but I think myself the happiest of missionaries.' 'Do you think that I care for my soul if my boy be gone to the fire?' cries the mother in Tennyson's 'Rizpah'. It is that same self-identifying love of which Jesus' baptism speaks.

In the great moment of Jesus' baptism, says the narrative, two things came to him – a Voice and a Vision. The Voice spoke to him out of heaven, and in the Vision of the dove the Holy Spirit descended. The Voice was the call for which, through the 'silent years' at Nazareth, he had been waiting, the call to his life-work; the Spirit was the equipment for obeying the call and for carrying out the work. 'Thou art my beloved Son, in whom I am well pleased' – that swept the last hesitation from Jesus' soul, and the Messianic vocation was accepted. And with the Vision came the endowment for Messiahship: the sense of power flooded his soul. The Spirit of God, which had been brooding over creation from the first (Genesis 1:2), haunting the dreams of saints (Psalm 139:7), and breaking out intermittently in the words of prophets (Isaiah 61:1), was now focused and concentrated to one burning point in Jesus' soul; and he came up from the water, the Called of the Father, the Power of God unto salvation.

V
The Desert

1 *The* BACKGROUND *of the* STORY

ONE or two preliminary questions meet us on the threshold of this story.

How did the story come to be in the Gospels at all? The Master's fight with Satan happened out in a desert, far from the beaten track and the eyes of men. During those forty days and nights Jesus was utterly alone, with not another soul anywhere near him, not a disciple or a friend or anyone to see what happened and tell the story afterwards. Yet the Evangelists are able to give a vivid and detailed account. How has that come about? Clearly there is only one explanation: the story came direct from the lips of Christ himself.

Why did Jesus tell it? That chapter of his life was closed: why did he go back to it and bring it to light? Certainly not to gratify anyone's curiosity. Certainly not to provide additional biographical materials for posterity or to supply an extra chapter in our Gospels. Probably there were two reasons. First, Jesus shared this experience with his disciples in order to help them through their own tempted hours. It does help greatly, as everyone who has ever been tempted knows, to hear of some other's fight and victory. And if that other should be Christ – how mightily it helps! But second, Jesus told this story because the titanic struggle of the desert days and nights had marked his soul for ever, and he could never forget. He could see and feel it after months as plainly as if it had happened only yesterday – the wild, desolate loneliness, the rocks and crags with the pitiless sun beating down on them by day and the biting night wind moaning across them in the dark, the prowling beasts, the famishing hunger, the demon voices whispering to his heart, the grace of God and the angels that had brought him through. Jesus told his disciples of it because he could not help it. It would not hide.

What does this imply about the Temptation? It means that Christ's temptation was real, literally desperately real. Now that needs to be said emphatically; for many people are quite sure that it was not and cannot have been real, at least not as our own familiar, dogged temptations are. That idea springs from a praiseworthy motive of doing honour to Jesus. 'Surely,' it is said, 'if Jesus was the Son of God, he must always have done the right thing without any struggle at all. The very possibility of inward conflict is excluded.' But is it? It may be glorifying Jesus to say he won his victory always without effort. But surely it is glorifying him far more to say he marched to it through an agony of sweat and blood.

And indeed the whole Gospel and our own hopes of salvation are bound up with a Christ who was 'tempted in all points' – not just here and there, but in all points – 'like as we are' (Hebrews 4:15). The dramatic story of it is told in a pictorial, symbolical way; but what we have to remember is that the experience itself was wholly inward. As we see Jesus then, we see him not with any great, gaunt, black-winged Satan beside him (as children's picture-books sometimes present the scene), not that at all: we see Jesus quite alone, sitting on a spur of rock, with his head bowed and his hands clenched, and then falling down on his knees, and then on his face, with a cry breaking from him that sounds like – 'Oh God, if it be possible, let this cup pass'; and then we turn our eyes away, for it is an awful thing to see the Son of God like that. The writer to the Hebrews settled it once and for all when he penned the brief, terrific words – 'He hath suffered, being tempted' (2:18).

When did this desert experience come? It came immediately after the Baptism. That is quite vital to an understanding of it. Indeed, it may be said that it was what happened at the Baptism that caused the Temptation. For there, down in the water of the Jordan, with the heavens opening above him and the voice of God speaking right home to his heart, Jesus had suddenly grown conscious of his Messianic power. He had come up out of the water with his whole being throbbing with that exultant discovery. And it was then the Tempter struck. This new, magnificent power – how was it to be used? All three temptations turn on that.

2 *The* FIRST TEMPTATION:
The SPIRITUAL *versus the* MATERIAL

Alone in the wilderness, after days and nights of prayer and meditation and fasting, Jesus was starving. And there was no help at hand, unless … – 'Make the stones bread!' said a sudden voice within.

Now that temptation attacked Jesus along three lines. *It attacked him along the line of his new-found power.* Would this not be a splendid chance to test that power, to see if it really worked, to prove whether it was something more than an imagination and a dream? 'Son of God' – but *was* he Son of God? 'Try it!' said Satan. 'Put it to the proof!'

It attacked him along the line of his vocation. God was needing Jesus for his work. God, he knew, had a tremendous mission waiting for him down the future years, and if he died out there in the desert with all that unfulfilled – what then? Would he not be defeating God? Would he not be robbing the world of its Messiah, and men of their salvation, and God of his Kingdom? Was it not his duty to save himself? 'Make the stones bread,' said Satan.

It attacked him along the line of his love for men. For surely it was not his own hunger alone that was in Jesus' thoughts in these desert days. There was the hunger of the great multitudes of the world's poor, the desperate, appalling need of the shepherdless hosts of Palestine and beyond who had barely enough to keep body and soul together. If he were the Son of God, ought he not, for their sakes, to make the stones bread? The question here was not one of an occasional gift of food to the hungry, such as the Evangelists subsequently record: it was a question of the regular method to be adopted for his whole public career. Ought he not to use his power to satisfy mankind's bodily needs, and so gain a short-cut to their affections? Then, after that, he would be able to do anything, absolutely anything, with them, to sweep whole grateful multitudes of them straight into the Kingdom of God! First the earthly Paradise, then the heavenly Paradise – was that not the right order? 'In the name of your compassion for men,' said the Tempter, 'make the stones bread.'

It was subtle, Satanically subtle. But Jesus refused. Why? We can discern two reasons. Just suppose he had consented. Suppose that, having eaten, and feeling now like a giant refreshed, he had turned his back on the desert and made for the crowded streets again, travelling in the greatness of his strength. What then? *Then Christ the brother and comrade would have been lost to us for ever.* For no longer would he have been standing shoulder to shoulder with us in our human pains and privations and troubles. Never again could we have sung:

Our fellow-suff'rer yet retains
A fellow-feeling of our pains;

And still remembers in the skies
His tears, his agonies, and cries.

It was in the name of his brotherhood with men that Jesus rejected the Tempter and hurled his suggestion back with scorn.

But again Jesus refused, *because he had come into the world to win men, not to bribe them.* That does not imply for a moment that Jesus was indifferent to people's material needs and social conditions. Indeed, he cared far more about these things than any reformer or politician or philanthropist who ever lived. Sometimes his followers have forgotten that. But we have been rediscovering it. We know now that until the cry for bread – and that includes the cry for a decent home and a clean environment and a Christianised social order – is answered, there can be no rest for Christ, and no rest for the Church, and no rest for any of us who call him Lord.

But our point just now is that when, in spite of all that, in spite of his passionate longing to see the earth a garden of God, Jesus refused the short-cut of making the stones bread, it was because he was in the world to win men, not to bribe them. He knew there was a hunger in the human heart deeper and stronger and more insistent than the hunger for bread and material things. And it was that deeper hunger, that nameless longing of the soul which can be satisfied, not with bread, nor riches, nor any material comforts whatsoever, but only with the broken body of God – it was that Christ came to appease. The Bread he gave was himself.

3 *The* SECOND TEMPTATION: *The* LURE *of the* SPECTACULAR

It is worth emphasising that there *was* a second temptation. It might have been thought that Jesus, having gained his victory once, had gained it for ever. But there too he shared our human experience: and we can remember for our comfort, when old beaten foes come back with stubborn doggedness, that Christ was tempted not once, not twice, but many times, and not only in the desert, but throughout his life.

There was a day, for example, months afterwards, when his best friend tried to save him from himself, and begged him for pity's sake to turn aside before it was too late and avoid the Cross (Matthew 16:22f). 'Be it far from thee, Lord,' said Peter, 'this shall not be unto thee.' Whereupon, says the Evangelist, Jesus suddenly turned round on Peter with the cry, 'Get thee behind me, Satan.' There is a note of tension in that which can only mean that Jesus was being tempted then almost more than he could bear. Even on Calvary the Tempter came again, and made a last desperate bid: 'If thou be the Son of God, come down from the cross' (Matthew 27:40). So Jesus, like ourselves, had to fight again and again. 'The devil departed from him,' says Luke significantly, *'for a season'* (4:13).

To understand the second temptation, remember that Jesus in the desert days and nights was thinking out his life-work and the methods he would follow. He knew that God had sent him to save the world. But how best to do it? Suppose he confined himself to preaching. Would they listen? Would they respond? It seemed doubtful, to say the least. It was then the Tempter struck in, suggesting another way, a far surer way. Why confine himself to the simple Gospel? Why not do some-thing startling, dramatic, spectacular? That would bring the world to his feet. So the wild idea of the leap from the Temple pinnacle broke upon his mind.

But Jesus rejected it. Why?

'Thou shall not tempt [make wilful proof of] *the Lord thy God'* (Matthew 4:7). That was one reason for his refusal. The spectacular leap would not have been an act of trust in God at all: it would have been flinging a challenge in God's face and

forcing God's hand. Jesus would not have anything to do with that. That, to Jesus, was sin.

Again, suppose he had done it – *would it really have effected its purpose?* Would it have saved a single soul? It would, no doubt, have brought forth an immediate burst of admiration and applause. It would certainly not have bound them to him for life. People may acclaim something that stirs their imagination; but they can be saved only by something that touches the heart.

Moreover, it was always against the grain with Jesus *to appeal to the lower side of men's nature and the sensationalist spirit*. People might want him to blaze his message across the skies, to stop the stars in their courses, to call down fire from heaven, to change the face of nature; but no one knew better than Christ that that spirit had absolutely nothing to do with religion at all. That was not the Messiah spirit, but the Herod spirit. (See Luke 23:8.)

Finally, *Jesus would never violate the freedom of men's wills*. The leap from the pinnacle would have involved that too. It would have been overriding their calmer judgement. It would have been forcing a confession of faith. That was one thing Jesus definitely would not do. If he could not win people into salvation by sheer goodness and love, he was not going to force them into it by miracles and magic. 'Behold, I stand at the door, and knock. *If any man open the door,* I will come in.'

4 *The* THIRD TEMPTATION: *The* WAY *of* COMPROMISE

Here, again, it is important to remember that it was the Master's life-work that was the issue. The passion of his life was to win the wide earth for God, to bind all the kingdoms of the world and the glory of them to God's great throne for ever. What the Tempter now suggested was that the easiest, quickest, surest way to do that would be to lower his demands from men, to haul down the flag of the faith a tiny bit, to come to terms with the world-powers. One moment kneeling at my feet, said Satan, and your dream will be true!

'Get thee hence!' Jesus rejected the compromise. Why? Because he knew it would be the death of religion to ask anything less than the whole.

Very nobly the early Church followed its Master there. It is an extraordinarily significant fact that of all the new religions that came pouring in to Rome out of the East in the early centuries, the religion of Jesus was the only one to arouse real persecution. When the religions of Osiris, Cybele, and other gods and goddesses came, Rome welcomed them all with open arms. But when the lonely God from Palestine came, and the Nazarene's name was first heard on the imperial streets, Rome girded herself to fight him to the death. Why? Because Osiris and the rest were content to live together and share the honours; but the young God with the nailprints in his hands would not live together or share the honours with any. From the day of Jesus' decision in the desert, the demand of his religion was all or nothing.

And from the day of that decision, Calvary was inevitable: a demand like that will always mean a Cross. Hence the fury with which Rome persecuted his followers, hunted them down to the catacombs, burned them in the arena, threw them to the lions, flung them outside the camp to bear Christ's reproach. It was because it was obedient to that decision in the desert that the Church, like its Lord, was crucified, dead, and buried; and it was because it was obedient to the decision that the Church, again like its Lord, broke the grave and went out conquering and to conquer. For the road which Jesus faced when he refused to compromise is the hard road, the long road, the sacrificial road; but it is the royal road to the Kingdom.

5 TWO PRACTICAL CONCLUSIONS

The study of the Temptation narrative illuminates two important points.

On the one hand, it proves that *temptation is not necessarily
sin*. Men like Peter and John might easily have been brought by
the persistence of their personal temptations almost to despair.
They had seen the vision splendid and had left all to follow it,
and yet temptations sprang upon them distressingly – until they
may well have questioned the reality of their own discipleship
and thought themselves tainted with ineradicable sin. But from
the moment when Jesus narrated this story to them, the sting
was taken out of that perplexity. For the thought of Jesus, the
fairest, cleanest, noblest soul in all the earth, yet carrying the
sweat of almost unbearable temptation upon his brow, settled it
once and for all (and it ought to settle it for troubled, sensitive
souls today): temptation is not sin.

On the other hand, the narrative illuminates the great saying
of a later disciple – '*In that he himself hath suffered being tempted,
he is able to succour them that are tempted*' (Hebrews 2:18). Peter and
John and the rest verified that anew every day they lived with
him. For as time went on, they found that they could conquer
the love of the world in themselves, and indeed every low love,
not by crushing it down by sheer force of will, but by having a
better love to set against it – the love of Jesus, who had gone the
same hard road himself. Contact with his radiant, dynamic personality achieved the impossible. God's own victorious power
was coming across into their weak lives, not through any moral
code, impersonal and cold and uninspiring, but through this
splendid, magnificent, adorable Lover of their souls; not by any
strained and difficult obedience, but by 'Christ in them the
hope of glory'. 'He is able,' they said.

That is the heart and centre of Christianity – yesterday, today,
and for ever.

VI
The Gospel of the Kingdom

1 *The* WATCHWORD

EVERY new idea that has burst upon the world has had a watch-word. Always there has been some word or phrase in which the very genius of the thing has been concentrated and focused, some word or phrase to blazon on its banners when it went marching out into the world. Islam had a watchword: 'God is God, and Mohammed is his prophet.' The French Revolution had a watchword: 'Liberty, Equality, Fraternity.' The democratic idea had a watchword: 'Government of the people, by the people, for the people.' The Student Volunteer Missionary Union had a watchword: 'The Evangelisation of the World in this Generation.' Every new idea that has stirred the hearts of people has created its own watchword, something to wave like a flag, to rally the ranks and win recruits. Now the greatest idea that has ever been born upon the earth is the Christian idea. And Christianity came with a watchword, magnificent and mighty and imperial. The watchword was: 'The Kingdom of God.'

Every great leader who has ever arisen has been possessed by one master-thought. Always there has been one thought that has gripped the person like a passion, one truth that has burned in his sky like a Greenland sun, never setting night or day. Socrates had a master-thought: the immortality of the soul. Buddha had a master-thought: the renunciation of life. Napoleon had a master-thought: the domination of Europe. Luther had a

THE GOSPEL OF THE KINGDOM

master-thought: the freedom of the individual. Every great leader who has towered up above the sons of men has had one thought that held and haunted and dominated him, one thought that drove a passage for him through this close-grained earth and lifted him high. Now the greatest Leader who ever led the hosts of humanity is Jesus Christ. And Jesus, like all these others, came with *his* master-thought, glorious and thrilling, world-shaking and world-transforming. Christ's master-thought was 'the Kingdom of God'.

In the Gospels themselves the name 'kingdom of God' occurs over a hundred times. The first sermon of Jesus' earthly ministry, says Mark, had this for its subject – 'The time is fulfilled, and the kingdom of God is at hand' (Mark 1:15). The last sermon of his earthly ministry had the same great theme, for when Jesus came back to his own for a time after Calvary, says the Book of Acts, he spoke to them 'of the things pertaining to the kingdom of God' (Acts 1:3). And if the beginning and the end of Christ's ministry struck that one note, it was also kept sounding all the way through. Think of the parables. How many of them begin: 'The kingdom of God is like … '! Think of Christ's commission to his followers: 'Into whatsoever city ye enter, say unto them, The kingdom of God is come nigh unto you' (Luke 10:10f). Here we have the watchword of the evangel. But what does it mean? What did Jesus mean by it? The trouble is that we are apt to read our own thoughts into it. We are apt to take out of it our own thoughts about religion. What we have to do is to ask, not what does the name 'kingdom of God' mean as popularly used today, not what do we think it ought to mean, but what did Jesus mean by it? That, and only that, is our concern now.

2 *The* KINGDOM *in* JUDAISM

First it will be well to get this clear, that while the thought was original with Jesus, the name itself was not. To Jewish ears, 'kingdom of God' has a familiar sound, and in Jewish writings it had a prominent place. To take only one instance out of many, there is the great cry that breaks out of the Book of Daniel (7:14): 'His dominion is an everlasting dominion, and his kingdom that which shall not be destroyed.'

Now to understand Jesus' position, it is important to observe that in the generation immediately before Jesus, two things had happened to this Jewish thought of the kingdom. On the one hand, it had suddenly become redoubled in intensity. That was the direct result of the foreign domination and oppression; for with Rome's heel on Israel's throat, the only hope was that God would strike in and make his kingdom come. On the other hand, it had been almost completely secularised. Material splendours, political aggrandisement, secular benefits – these were the things on which the popular mind was set, and all spiritual expectations were swamped. Even the men Jesus chose for his disciples found it hard to break away from the prevailing secularism; and when James and John demanded the best places in the kingdom (Matthew 20:20), or when after the Resurrection the disciples asked, 'Lord, wilt thou at this time restore again the kingdom to Israel?' (Acts 1:6), it showed how deeply-rooted the earthly, political, unspiritual ideas of the kingdom were. In short, the 'kingdom of God' had come to be the slogan of Jewish nationalism.

Subsequent history shows how strong and unquenchable the nationalist spirit can be. We think of a Mazzini in Italy, a Sun Yat-sen in China, a Gandhi in India, each of them fostering the nationalist spirit and fanning it to a blaze. Certainly that spirit has a real part to play in the evolution of the race. But, equally certainly, God never meant it to be an end in itself. Over and above the sentiment of nationality, God looks to his people to develop a fellowship that will be supra-national, non-exclusive, world-embracing.

Never in the whole course of history has the nationalist spirit been stronger than in the Judaism of Jesus' day. 'How is it,' a woman once said to Jesus, 'that thou, being a Jew, askest drink of me, which am a woman of Samaria?' And the Evangelist adds the explanatory note – 'The Jews have no dealings with the Samaritans' (John 4:9). That was what Jewish nationalism had become. It had entrenched itself even in the Temple, the last place surely where it ought to have intruded. There, between the outer court of the Gentiles and the inner court of the Jews, stood a barrier with this written on it – 'Let no foreigner enter within. Whosoever is taken so doing will himself be the cause that death overtakes him.' And when the Jewish mind dreamed of its Messiah, it was a kind of super Judas Maccabaeus they envisaged, driving his way with drawn sword to the throne of an earthly kingdom. Indeed, in the name 'kingdom of God', nearly all the emphasis was being thrown upon 'kingdom', and very little of it upon 'God'. Only the name was there, awaiting the day when it would be re-born and baptised into Christ.

That day arrived. Jesus found this name waiting. He took it, transformed it beyond all recognition, and made it central in his message. Jesus put so much into it, and brought out so many different aspects of it, that it is difficult to reduce his meaning to any single formula or definition. But clearly there were two main lines along which all his thoughts of the kingdom ran. On the one hand, he thought of it as the rule of God in the heart. On the other hand, he thought of it as the rule of God in the world. Let us take these two aspects separately.

3 *The* KINGDOM *as the* RULE *of* GOD *in the* HEART

When Jesus proclaimed this and made it a foundation stone of his Gospel, he was really drawing three vital distinctions, every one of which laid the axe to the root of prevailing, popular conceptions. If the kingdom was the rule of God in the heart, it followed, first, that the kingdom of God was moral, not nationalistic; second, that the kingdom of God was spiritual, not material; third, that the kingdom of God was actual, not ideal.

(1) *It is moral, not nationalistic.* Jesus told his fellow-countrymen bluntly that they had mistaken their enemy. They thought their enemy was Rome, the foreign legions that went marching up and down the highways of the land they loved. Jesus told them that the enemy whom they ought to fear and fight was the devil, the legions of evil that go marching through the sanctities of the soul. Again and again he came back to that. 'How can one enter into a strong man's house,' he said, 'and spoil his goods, except he first bind the strong man? Then he will spoil his house' (Matthew 12:29). Who was the 'strong man' Jesus was thinking of there? Not Caesar – but Satan. And Jesus added that if, up and down the land, broken lives were being healed and devils cast out, it was a sign that he, the Christ of God, had already bound up the strong man, that the kingdom of Satan was now breaking up, and the kingdom of God coming into its own.

But never did Jesus make this clearer than when he stood before Pilate. 'My kingdom is not of this world,' he said. 'If my kingdom were of this world, then would my servants fight; but now is my kingdom not from hence' (John 18:36). And it is one of history's most curious anomalies that whereas Rome, acting in the person of Pilate, crucified Jesus ostensibly at least because she could not allow the setting up of any rival earthly kingdom, and it was represented that that was what Jesus was seeking to do, the Jews, on the other hand, crucified Jesus because they *did* want passionately to see an earthly kingdom set up, and knew now that that was the one thing Jesus was determined *not* to do. 'My kingdom is not of this world' – that signed the death-warrant of Jewish nationalism, but it signed Jesus' death-warrant too. 'Away with him,' they cried, 'this King who will not rule!' But Christ's rule, which is God's rule, is in the heart. It is in the secret places of our moral life. The kingdom, said Jesus, is moral, not nationalistic.

(2) *It is spiritual, not material.* It was not only an earthly kingdom on which the Jews had set their hearts. It was also an age of material good things. God's kingdom would lift them out of want and struggle, and set them down amongst the good things of this life.

Now you will remember that there was actually a point in Jesus' life when he considered the possibility of making use of that material hope in God's service. 'Make the stones bread!' said the Tempter. 'Appeal to men along the lower line first, and then they will be ready for the higher. Start by making them comfortable – then they will have an ear for the Gospel.' But Jesus turned that suggestion down. That, he said, would only obscure his message and complicate his challenge. For the kingdom of God was not meat and drink, but righteousness, and peace, and joy in the Holy Ghost (Romans 14:17).

Translated into today's terms, this means that all the social reform in the world, *taken by itself,* will never bring in the kingdom; that there is a primary and essential work of God's grace in the inner person for which no amount of amelioration of his outward circumstances can possibly act as a substitute; that you will never make a Utopia out of regenerate conditions but unregenerate hearts, nor build the City of God out of those who have never been converted and redeemed. Admittedly, true religion has mighty social reactions, and it is those who have themselves found God who will be the first to join every crusade for the betterment of human conditions: get the spiritual side of things right, and you will assuredly be helping to put the material side right. (On this, see chapter XV: 'Jesus and Social Questions'). But the fact we have been insisting on remains.

'The kingdom,' said Jesus, 'cometh not with observation. It is within you' (Luke 17:20f): meaning, 'It is now in your midst, in the new age God is inaugurating.'

(3) *It is actual, not ideal*. The Jews could only dream of the kingdom: Jesus said it was already here. They could only cast longing eyes into a dim, ideal future: Jesus said it had arrived on earth, and was a present reality. One Sabbath, in the synagogue of his home-town of Nazareth, he read aloud to the assembled people the great prophecy of Isaiah in which the blessed coming of the kingdom was forecast – how the broken-hearted would be healed, the captives delivered, the blind given their sight; and then, closing the book, he began – 'This day is this fulfilled in your ears!' (Luke 4:21ff). And another day when talking in private to his disciples, 'Blessed,' he said, 'are the eyes which see the things that ye see' – things for which kings and prophets of old times yearned, and peered down the dark future, and strained their eyes to see, and yet never saw – but ye see them, the splendours of the kingdom!' (Luke 10:23f). Again and again in the Gospels, Jesus strikes homes to people's hearts with this amazing discovery – that the kingdom they dream about has in some sense arrived, is here now for those whose eyes are open and whose spiritual vision is cleansed. The kingdom, said Jesus, is actual, not ideal.

'Where is the Church,' cried a gallant Scots Covenanter in the days of persecution, when the flock of Christ was scattered over moor and glen, 'where is the Church of God in Scotland at this day? I will tell you where the Church is. It is wherever a praying young man or woman is at a dykeside in Scotland: that's where the Church is.' So if we ask, Where is the kingdom of God today? – here is the Gospel answer: it is wherever a man or woman has made Christ the Lord of life and accepted the rule of God in the heart. That is where the kingdom is. And that is the real explanation of the sudden happiness that comes to any one who makes the great decision: it is the other world, the eternal kingdom world, breaking through into time, coming above the surface in that person's life. The kingdom of God is there.

4 *The* KINGDOM *as the* RULE *of* GOD *in the* WORLD

There was a second main line along which Christ's thought of the kingdom ran. It was the rule of God in the heart; but it was also *the rule of God in the world.* Here, again, Christ was drawing three great distinctions. If the kingdom was the rule of God in the world, it followed, first, that the kingdom of God was social, not individualistic; second, that the kingdom of God was universal, not local; third, that the kingdom of God was awaiting a final consummation, and not yet fully complete.

(1) *It is social, not individualistic.* The very name implies this. It was to be *a kingdom.* It might indeed have its roots in solitary, separate souls that had been redeemed (religion always has its roots there), but its aim was nothing less than a redeemed society, a new order of humanity, a family fellowship, the sons and daughters of God. As this was Christ's programme and manifesto, it follows (and the united testimony of the Gospels makes this clear) that any religion which consists merely or mainly in getting one's own soul saved, which begins and ends in that, is something quite different from Christ's religion, something far inferior to Christ's religion, which never countenanced individualism run riot or the parochialism of a self-centred salvation. If there is a place in Christianity for desperate concern about one's own soul (and most certainly there is), there is also a place for this:

> *I will not cease from mental fight,*
> *Nor shall my sword sleep in my hand,*

Till we have built Jerusalem
   In England's green and pleasant land.

The kingdom, said Jesus, is the rule of God in the world: it is social, not individualistic.

(2) *It is universal, not local.* 'The field is the world,' said Jesus, describing the ground on which the Gospel seed was to be sown (Matthew 13:38). Again, telling his men of their high responsibility as Christians, he said, 'Ye are the salt' – but of what? Not of the Church, not of their own families, not of any one class or sect or party – 'Ye are the salt of the earth'! (Matthew 5:13). And again, describing the magnetic force of the evangel with which they were charged – 'They shall come from the east, and from the west, and from the north, and from the south, and shall sit down in the kingdom of God' (Luke 13:29).

Never did Jesus think of God's kingdom as an ark of refuge for the few, to which they could escape with a sigh of relief from a ruined world. Jesus came, not to snatch a few elect souls out of a lost and hopeless world: he came to save the world. Hence any Church which is content to minister to the few who are saved already, to carry them at last safe to their desired haven, and just leave all the rest, is definitely failing Christ. The Church is here under Christ, to claim nothing less than the whole world for God's kingdom; and all the spiritual forces of the unseen are backing up the people who are pledged to that mighty imperialism. The kingdom, said Jesus, is universal, not local.

(3) *The Kingdom awaits a final consummation, and is not yet complete.* Here is the great paradox of it, that it is both present and future; present because (as we have seen) it is there now wherever there is a fully surrendered heart; but also future, because the crowning glory is still to come. 'When the Son of Man shall come in his glory,' said Jesus, looking past the present order of things to some terrific act of God that would usher in

the consummation, 'then shall the King say, Come, ye blessed of my Father, inherit the kingdom' (Matthew 25:31ff). And whatever else that mighty Second Advent hope that glowed and blazed in Jesus' soul may mean, we know that at least it does mean this – that when man has done everything that he can do to build the everlasting kingdom, it is God, and God alone, who can make that kingdom perfect; that somehow and somewhere, in ways beyond our present comprehension, God is going to come breaking in triumphantly; that the age-long warfare between good and evil is not to drag on and on indefinitely as an indecisive warfare, but that one day it is going to end, and end in the victory of God, and on that day the last enemy will be dead beneath Christ's feet for ever.

That was the winning note that Jesus struck. That was the eternal hope he gave the world, signed with his own name and guarantee. That was what generated the great vision of the seer with whose book the New Testament closes (Revelation 11:15), the vision of a day when heaven itself would ring with a mighty tumult of voices, and their adoring, rejoicing cry would be this – 'The kingdoms of this world are become the kingdom of our Lord, and of his Christ; and he shall reign for ever and ever.'

VII
The First Twelve

1 *The* YOUTH *of the* DISCIPLES

CHRISTIANITY began as a young people's movement. In thinking of Jesus and his disciples, that is the first fact to make quite clear. Unfortunately, it is a fact which Christian art and Christian preaching have too often obscured. But it is quite certain that the original disciple band was a young men's group. Most of the Apostles were probably still in their twenties when they went out after Jesus.

In this connection, notice how St Paul, writing almost a generation later, reports that of the five hundred to whom the risen Christ appeared, 'the greater part remain unto this present' (I Corinthians 15:6): the natural inference is that the spiritual conquests of Jesus had been mainly among the younger people. Note also in the Gospels themselves the Master's forms of address to his followers. We find the Greek word *tekna*, meaning 'children', and sometimes the affectionate diminutive *teknia* (John 13:33); or *paidia* (John 21:5), 'my dear children', or as we might put it today (Dr Moffatt translates it thus), 'lads'.

Jesus himself, we should not forget, went out to his earthly ministry with 'the dew of his youth' upon him (Psalm 110:3 – this Psalm was applied to Jesus, first by himself, and then by the Apostolic Church). It was a true instinct that led the Christians of a later day, when they drew the likeness of their Master on the walls of the catacombs, to portray him, not old and weary and broken with pain, but as a young shepherd out on the hills of the morning. The original version of Isaac Watts' great hymn was true to fact: 'When I survey the wondrous Cross, Where *the young Prince* of glory died.' And no one has ever understood the heart of youth – in its gaiety and gallantry and generosity and hope, its sudden loneliness and haunting dreams, hidden conflicts and strong temptations – as Jesus has. And no one ever realised more clearly than Jesus that the adolescent years of life, when strange dormant thoughts are stirring and the whole world begins to unfold, are God's best chance with the soul. When Jesus and youth come together, deep calls to deep. There is an immediate, instinctive feeling of kinship, and everything that is fine and noble and pure in youth bows down in admiration and adoration before him.

It is not surprising then that Christianity entered the world as a young people's movement. When we study the story of the first Twelve, it is a young men's adventure we are studying. We see them following their Leader out into the unknown, not knowing very clearly who he is, or why they are doing it, or where he is likely to lead them; they are just magnetised by him, fascinated and gripped and held by something irresistible in the soul of him, laughed at by friends, plotted against by foes, with doubts sometimes growing clamourous in their own hearts, until they almost wished they were well out of the whole business; yet still clinging to him, coming through the ruin of their hopes to a better loyalty, and earning triumphantly at last the great name the *Te Deum* gives them, 'The glorious company of the Apostles'. It is worth watching them, for we too may catch the infection of their spirit, and fall into step with Jesus.

2 DIVERSITY *of* CHARACTER

One of the most striking features of the first disciple-group

was the diversity of character it contained, an amazing syn-
thesis of humanly irreconcilable elements. Isaiah's vision of the
wolf and the lamb dwelling together was surely near fulfilment
when Simon the Zealot, the fiery nationalist, went arm-in-arm
with Matthew, the tax-gatherer and publican! Only one thing
could explain that strange union: they had each found Jesus.
Here was Peter, all energy, activity and impetuosity; here was
John, meditative, thoughtful and prayerful. That difference,
too, was transcended: they had each found Jesus. Here was
Andrew, a man of shining, untroubled faith; here was Thomas,
with his constitutional melancholy. They, too, were one now:
they had each found Jesus. The very composition of that first
group of Twelve is a mighty witness to the universality of Jesus.

In this point of diversity of character, the first group was a
microcosm of the Church that was to be. 'I, if I be lifted up
from the earth, will draw all men unto me,' said Jesus (John
12:32). He has done it, and is doing it – drawing people of
every generation and century, for Jesus alone never goes out
of date; of every race and country, so even Rudyard Kipling's
unbridgeable gulf between East and West is in Christ Jesus
bridged once and for all; people of every calling and vocation;
people of every temperament and disposition; people of every
class and party; people as diverse as Francis of Assisi and John
Bunyan, John Wesley and John Henry Newman, Brother
Lawrence and Aggrey of Africa, D L Moody and Temple
Gairdner. The City of God, says Revelation, has gates facing
to every point of the compass (21:13): they all lead to Christ.

3 *The* MASTER'S TWO-FOLD AIM

What was Jesus' purpose in selecting these men for special
discipleship? St Mark has put it into one short, significant
sentence: 'He ordained twelve, that they should be with him,

and that he might send them forth to preach' (Mark 3:14). That sentence is worth pondering: *'That they should be with him'* – it suggests, does it not, that Jesus, on the human side of his nature, felt the need of human fellowship and sympathy? The Gospels are full of lonely people – the Virgin Mary, the friendless lepers, the man at the pool of Bethesda, Judas, Pilate, and many others; but in a sense the loneliest figure of all on the Gospel page is the Christ himself. And often when the world outside had been showing itself callous and hostile and contemptuous, often when the day had brought him sneers that stung, or a studied indifference that was like a blow in the face, he would turn back at nightfall with a great relief to these twelve men who, for all their faults and bungling, did love him and did believe in him. As Jesus himself expressed it, one day when the end was near – 'It is you who have stood by me through my trials' (Luke 22:28, Moffatt). And still today, the love and trust of ordinary people mean more to Jesus than we might ever guess. 'If any man open the door, I will come in.'

'That they should be with him.' It was not only that the Saviour felt the need of human love and sympathy. It was also his purpose to train these men by fellowship with himself. Living with him every day, watching him in all kinds of situations, listening to his private talk, being admitted to his dreams and aspirations and hopes, they would end up by sharing his very spirit, would gradually come to see things with his eyes, and understand with his wonderfully understanding heart, and be fired with his own authentic fire. In short, the fellowship would make them real men of God. It is the best and simplest way of making real men and women of God today. Intimacy with Jesus is the best of all teachers.

'And that he might send them forth to preach.' The work in Galilee was growing so rapidly, and the opportunity was so great, and the need of perishing souls so desperate, that Jesus could not keep the work of evangelisation in his own hands.

The twelve men were chosen to carry and to pass on the torch that Jesus had kindled. That is one reason why we call the Church 'the Body of Christ'.

> *For Christ has no hands but our hands to do his work today,*
> *He has no feet but our feet to lead men in his way,*
> *He has no tongue but our tongues to tell men how he died,*
> *He has no help but our help to bring them to his side.*

'Apostle' means 'one who is sent forth'; no one can be a true 'disciple' if he or she is not prepared to be an 'apostle' too. Christ counts on you. Nineteen hundred years ago a group of young people under Christ changed the world. He is counting on young men and women today to do it again. 'Let no man,' said Martin Luther, 'lose the faith that God willeth to do a great work through him.'

4 *The* MASTER'S CALL

How were the first twelve recruits enrolled? No doubt to each of them the final call when it came was quite sudden and abrupt and decisive, but it seems likely that in every case a longer or shorter period of acquaintance with Jesus, and even companionship, had gone before and prepared the way. Indeed, there were probably three stages on the road to full apostleship. To begin with, they were simply his friends, remaining in their own homes and at their various secular activities, but seeing him and speaking with him from time to time. The second stage came with the sundering of home ties and the relinquishing of ordinary occupations. Finally there came the day when, from the main body of the followers who had gathered round him, twelve were set apart for the closest intimacy and the most vital work. The call to apostleship was then complete.

The apparent duplicating in the Gospels of the accounts of the calling of the disciples has often been felt to be a problem. But the above explanation provides a solution. Thus, for example, when we find one account of Peter's call in John 1:42, another different account in Luke 5:10f, and still another in Mark 3:13-16, it is not necessary to say that only one of the three narratives can be authentic and the others must be eliminated. The fact is they all have a true place in the story. For each represents a distinct stage in Peter's progress from his first acquaintance with Jesus to his full surrender. It was really a three-fold call: first the call to friendship, then the call to following, and finally the call to the full ministry of apostleship.

5 *The* TWELVE MEN

Look now at some of the men Jesus chose. One of them, Andrew, has become Scotland's patron saint. Whether the legends connecting Andrew and Scotland have any truth in them, we do not know: however, Scotland has a patron saint to be proud of. *Andrew* is a Greek word meaning 'brave', or 'manly', and the name describes the man. It was not an easy part Andrew had to play in the Gospel story. You will observe that he is generally described as 'Simon Peter's brother', and it is not an easy thing to be continually eclipsed by someone else's brilliance, and to have to stand in the shadow, even when that someone else is a brother. Andrew found Jesus before Peter: without Andrew, there might never have been a Peter in Christian history at all. Yet he had to stand and see Peter admitted to an intimacy (the inmost circle consisted of Peter, James and John), which he was never privileged to share. It was a real test of the man. And he came through with flying colours. Andrew had not one particle of envy in his whole nature.

Andrew was one of the young men who had been deeply

stirred by John the Baptist's revival movement. It was through that movement he was first brought into contact with Jesus. 'Behold the Lamb of God,' the Baptist had said, pointing to someone walking one evening alone by the river (John 1:36). Andrew and his friend, not knowing why, went after that solitary figure. 'Where dwellest thou?' 'Come and see.' And what would we not have given for a record of the conversation in that humble lodging that night, when Jesus and these two young men were alone together from four in the afternoon to dusk, and from dusk to dark, and from dark to the late, deep hour when the candles were at last put out! At any rate, after that, Andrew was Christ's man through and through.

It is an exceedingly significant fact that wherever Andrew appears on the Gospel scene, he is busy introducing someone else to Jesus. It began the very next morning, when he broke in on his brother Simon with that glad *'Eureka!* I have found the Christ!' 'And he brought him to Jesus' (John 1:42). When a famished crowd had followed the Master into the desert, it was Andrew who found the lad with the loaves (John 6:8f): and he brought him to Jesus. When the Greek strangers appealed to Philip for an introduction to his Master, it was to Andrew that Philip went for advice (John 12:20-22): and he brought them to Jesus. Andrew is not only the patron saint of Scotland, he is the patron saint of all missionary workers for ever. And that is still the disciple's calling – to bring someone else to Christ.

Peter was a born leader and the natural spokesman of the disciple-group. When Jesus, watching the crowds dwindling, put the question, 'Will ye also go away?', it was Peter who burst out, 'Lord, to whom shall we go? Thou hast the words of eternal life' (John 6:68). When the first great Christian confession came, it was Peter who made it: 'Thou art the Christ, the Son of the living God' (Matthew 16:16). When the broken-hearted band reassembled after Calvary, it was Peter who took the initiative: 'I go a fishing.' 'We also go with thee'

(John 21:3). Gallant, generous, affectionate, impetuous soul that he was, he was a born leader of men. But he had the defects of his qualities. It was to Peter that 'Get thee behind me, Satan' was said (Matthew 16:23). It was Peter who blurted out his mercenary question, 'Behold, we have forsaken all, and followed thee; what shall we have therefore?' (Matthew 19:27). It was Peter who disowned Christ at the jibe of a servant-lass (Matthew 26:69ff). What a moral mixture the human heart can be! Peter's story is quite familiar. It is our story too.

Yet 'Peter', Christ's name for Simon, means 'the Rock'. Jesus was looking into the future and seeing the mighty man of God that his bungling disciple was going to be. And what really turned Peter from shifting sand into a rock was the discovery that, after his tragic failure, Jesus believed in him still (Mark 16:7). 'Thou knowest all things; thou knowest that I love thee.' 'Feed my sheep' (John 21:17).

A famous legend of Peter's last days in Rome has come to us. Fleeing from the city in sudden panic, he met Jesus entering. *'Quo vadis, Domine?'* ('Wither goest thou, Master?') he asked. 'I go to Rome to be crucified a second time for thee,' was the answer. Whereupon Peter turned and went back with firm step to the martyr-death awaiting him. And so this 'Mr Valiant' of the early Church crossed the river. 'And all the trumpets sounded for him on the other side.'

In the inner circle of Christ's followers were the two sons of Zebedee, James and John. About James little is known. Only in two incidents in the Gospel does he appear, and both times it is in his brother's company. But his ineffaceable title to honour lies in this: that he was the protomartyr of the apostolic band (see Acts 12:2). John we may call the Jonathan of the New Testament: what Jonathan was to David in the Old Testament, that was John to the great Son of David in the New. 'My knights,' says Tennyson's Arthur, 'are sworn to vows of utter hardihood, utter gentleness': and in John that manly strength and womanly tenderness seem to have been perfectly united. It stands eternally to John's credit that he was there on Calvary to the last, and that it was of him that the words fell from Jesus' dying lips, 'Woman, behold thy son!' (John 19:26). No doubt there was another side to his nature, too; a less pleasing side, which comes out in three Gospel incidents – his rebuke to the unknown healer (Mark 9:38), his threat of fire to the recalcitrant Samaritan village (Luke 9:54), and his ambition for the best place in the kingdom (Mark 10:35ff). But the deepest thing in his nature was his passionate love for Jesus that was like a flame in his heart. And wherever the Gospel is preached, one great name, 'the disciple whom Jesus loved', will be told as a memorial to him.

One disciple, to whom history has done less than full justice, is Thomas: generally called Thomas the Doubter, the Agnostic, or even the Sceptic. That is hardly fair. It is worth remembering that when Jesus was setting his face towards Jerusalem and most of the disciples were protesting loudly against what seemed to them sheer reckless folly (John 11:8), one brave, quiet voice spoke up – 'Let us also go, that we may die with him' (John 11:16). If doubts did overshadow his soul (John 14:5; 20:25), they were certainly not the doubts of defiant scepticism. Rather they were just the penalty of his temperament, in which a touch of melancholy was mingled. And it is a great thing that, in the end, the finest confession of faith in the New Testament comes from this soul that fought its way through the mists and shadows to the light – 'My Lord and my God' (John 20:28).

Matthew was 'sitting at the receipt of custom' when Jesus called him (Matthew 9:9). To be a *publicanus,* or tax-gatherer, was to be hopelessly stigmatised in the eyes of every loyal Jew; the surprise in Capernaum that night must have been great when it was rumoured who the Rabbi's latest recruit was. This was the kind of friendship by which Jesus, to quote St Paul, 'made himself of no reputation' (Philippians 2:7). But neither Matthew nor Jesus took heed of anything the crowd might say. That night Matthew gave a feast for his friends (a strange company), with Jesus as his guest of honour (Matthew 9:10). Probably the converted tax-gatherer had three main motives in giving the feast. It was to celebrate his spiritual birthday; to provide an opportunity for an open confession of his new allegiance, which would mean committing himself publicly and irrevocably to Jesus and burning his boats behind him, so that there could be no going back to the old life; and it was to give his friends a chance of meeting Jesus and sharing his own wonderful experience. The name 'Friend of publicans and sinners' was first flung at Christ as a jibe, but it is his crowning glory now.

Little is known of five of the remaining six disciples, namely Philip, the earnest inquirer (see John 1:43ff; 14:8f); Simon, the Zealot and fiery nationalist; Bartholomew, who is probably to be identified with Nathanael (John 1:45ff); Lebbaeus, 'whose surname was Thaddaeus' (Matthew 10:3), who also had the name Judas (not Iscariot), and who is known to us by one single remark (John 14:22); and James the son of Alphaeus, of whom nothing at all is told. There remains only the dark enigma of the group, Judas Iscariot, 'who betrayed him'. We cannot enter into the problem of Judas here. Suffice to say, Jesus must have seen in Judas at one time the makings of a real apostle, or else he would never have chosen him; and that Judas must have been attracted and fascinated by Jesus, or else he would never have left everything to follow him. We shall try to probe the mystery of Judas later on (see chapter XVII, 'The Last Days').

Jesus chose these twelve men and set out to conquer the earth with them. An absurd adventure? Humanly speaking, yes, but God was in it: 'God hath chosen the weak things of the world, to confound the things which are mighty; and base things of the world, and things which are despised, hath God chosen, yea, and things which are not, to bring to nought things that are' (I Corinthians 1:27f).

VIII
The Teaching Method of Jesus

1   JESUS *as* TEACHER

WHEN Nicodemus came to Jesus by night, he opened the conversation with the words, 'We know that thou art *a teacher come from God*' (John 3:2); and history has echoed his verdict. The teaching of Jesus, even though great multitudes throughout the world are still outside its sphere, even though many of his own followers have never cared or never dared to put it fully into practice, has had a power and an effect with which the influence of no other teacher can even for a moment be compared. He stands alone – the Great Teacher. Readers of the Gospels cannot but be impressed by the large proportion of his time and strength which Jesus deliberately dedicated to the ministry of teaching. Clearly, then, it is of the utmost importance that we should study the teaching method of Jesus. How did he frame his lessons? How did he make contact with his hearers? How did he present his truths? How did he get his results? Questions like these are vital not only in view of the remarkable interest in the question of teaching methods in general at the present time, and the thoroughgoing revolution in method which recent years have witnessed: quite apart from that, they open up for us a new window into the mind of the Master himself.

It is necessary, however, in speaking of the teaching method of Jesus, to make, right at the outset, two qualifications. First, the word 'method' must not here be taken as suggesting a carefully enunciated and formulated system. The leading feature of all Jesus' teaching was its spontaneity and freedom. It was above all rules. And second, let us never forget that while Jesus was a teacher, a born teacher and a Prince of teachers, he was also far more than a teacher. It is no exaggeration to say, and it cannot be too strongly put, that if we possessed the whole bulk of Jesus' New Testament teaching, *and nothing more than that,* the world today would still be perishing as surely as if he had never come. For he himself is far more than his teaching; and it is not the teaching of Christ that saves, but the Christ who teaches. Dr Dale was right on the mark when he said, very memorably, that Jesus came not so much to preach the Gospel as rather that there might be a Gospel to preach.

But keeping these two considerations in mind, we can now face our subject. For the sake of clearness, let us follow two lines of inquiry. What were the particular features of Jesus' teaching method? And what were its general principles?

2 *The* PARTICULAR FEATURES *of* JESUS' TEACHING METHOD

The first feature to be noticed is a very obvious one: *it was oral teaching.* It was spoken, not written. Indeed, only once in the Gospels do we see Jesus writing, and then it was in the sand he wrote (John 8:6). All his precious, golden words, all his final pronouncements on faith and morals, all his 'oracles of God', were trusted to the memories of a group of Galilean peasants and fisherfolk.

Was it not a risk? Was there not a danger that the winds of the years might carry his words away, and all he had taught be lost? No. For Jesus knew (and in many a parable he came back to this) that once you have planted a seed, you can leave it to look after itself: God and the soil will do the rest. He knew that once he had planted his words in human hearts, he could confidently leave them there: they would haunt mankind down the years, and would live for ever. No need for him to write his teaching down; that teaching, once let loose upon the earth, would make its way by its own inherent power and march deathlessly across the ages.

Ibsen, in his *Emperor and Galilean*, puts a soliloquy into the fourth century Emperor Julian's mouth. 'Where is he now? Has he been at work elsewhere since *that* happened at Golgotha? Where is he now? What if he goes on and on, suffers and dies and conquers again and again, from world to world?' That has been the story of the words of Jesus.

A second notable feature of Jesus' method lies in the fact that *much of his profoundest teaching was elicited by quite casual incidents and events.* That is to say, it was largely unpremeditated, aimed at the particular circumstances of the moment, and addressed to a specific situation. An encounter with a paralytic in the synagogue (Matthew 12:10), a wayside interview with a young aristocrat (Matthew 19:16), a sudden quarrel among his disciples (Luke 9:46), a debate on the vexed question of the imperial taxation (Matthew 22:17) – these are instances of the particular situations out of which much of the Master's teaching arose.

Now it might be thought that teaching like this was bound to be purely local and temporal in its application, and therefore not valid for us today. Nothing could be further from the truth. In point of fact, it is precisely because so much of Jesus' teaching was of that apparently incidental nature, addressed directly to the passing needs of the moment, that it does still hold good. Anything systematic in the doctrine or philosophy would, no doubt, have perished long ago; but these flashing words, because they struck straight home to the urgent needs of the actual men and women whom Jesus met and talked with, remain valid for ever. Systems of thought are continually changing from age to age, but the human heart, with its problems and perplexities, does not change; human temptations today are still as tempting, and human tears as bitter, as when Satan whispered in Simon Peter's soul or Mary Magdalene wept at Jesus' feet. It is because Christ spoke to immediate, definite needs that his teaching now belongs to all the world.

A third feature to be noticed is this: *always Jesus' teaching was adapted to his audience.* The first thing he did was to put himself at the point of view of his hearers, and to start from that. Was the law of Moses their working religion? Then with the law of Moses Jesus would begin, and go on from that to the better law of God. Was it a national kingdom they were dreaming of for Israel? Then Jesus would meet them on that ground, and lead them on to a spiritual kingdom. Always he began where his hearers were.

Hence the wonderful simplicity of his language. Direct and simple and forceful, that language – so unlike the speech of the professional religion of his day – had a grip and an appeal from which men could not get away. And he never went too fast. He never rushed his pupils. Step by step he led them. 'I have yet many things to say unto you,' he once told them, 'but ye cannot bear them now' (John 16:12). With divine reserve and reticence he would keep back part of the revelation (his own Sonship of God, for example) until his hearers were able to receive it.

The practical issue of this for today ought to be stressed. It never was Christ's way to demand a fully-fledged faith for a beginning. It was not his way to hold men back from discipleship on the grounds of an incomplete creed. Quite certainly that is not his way today. He puts himself alongside his brethren. He bids them attach themselves to him at any point they can. He takes them on with the faith that they can offer him. He is content with that as a beginning; and from that he leads his friends on, as he led the first group on, step by step, to the utmost secret of who he is, and to the full glory of discipleship.

One other particular feature of his method is very apparent: namely *the figurative element in his teaching*. By his illustrations, his epigrams, his paradoxes, and above all, by his parables – those matchless pictures which are not only creations of purest artistry but also living revelations of grace, windows opening suddenly upon life and destiny and God – he made people actually *see* the truths which he was proclaiming. Very often, while Jesus was speaking, some sudden picture would flash its way across his hearers' minds, so that even those whom no amount of abstract reasoning or argument would have convinced were left crying, 'I see it! I see it!' Many were ready to confess that until they met Jesus they had been blind, drifting through life like people with their eyes shut, more than half asleep, never guessing at life's glory; now, thanks to him, they were awake and alive, seeing life and seeing God. Jesus was the world's great giver of *vision*.

3 *The* GENERAL PRINCIPLES *of* JESUS' TEACHING METHOD

Turning now from the particular features of Jesus' method to its general principles, we notice, first, that *it was authoritative teaching*. 'The people,' says Matthew, 'were astonished at his doctrine, for he taught them as one having authority, and not as the scribes' (Matthew 7:28f). With Jesus, there was no 'perhaps', or 'it may be so', or 'I rather think so'; no speculation or guesswork or fumbling or faltering, but 'Verily I say unto you' rung out with the assurance of God himself. 'Not as the scribes' – for the scribes relied slavishly on tradition: 'Thus saith Moses', 'Thus saith Rabbi X', 'Thus saith the law and the prophets', never daring to speak in their own name.

In other words, it was all second-hand religion. And the fact that it was second-hand could not be hid. Even the common people who listened to them knew it was second-hand, and felt the unreality of it, and despised it in their hearts. What Emerson says of Seneca might well be applied to the scribes: 'His thoughts are excellent if only he had the right to utter them', for they were talking of things they had never experienced. But into that there burst this new voice out of Galilee – 'It was said by them of old time ... but I say unto you' – with one stroke sweeping scribism and all its buttressed positions aside, striking down through all the layers of tradition to bedrock fact, to the living God. And people were left gasping at the sheer daring of it, amazed and overwhelmed by the marvellous assurance of it – but also feeling with a great thrill of the heart that here was the real thing at last, here was a man who had seen what he was talking about, and knew it and had a right to speak, a man straight from God!

It should be stressed that here again we are dealing with something not local and temporal in its significance, but universal and permanent. Our own age, which has seen the breaking up of so many old and cherished traditions and the issuing of a new challenge to authority in so many spheres – in morals and religion, no less than in politics and society – is not, as some would suggest, left without chart or compass: *the Christ still stands.* To heart, and mind, and conscience, his teaching still authenticates itself as the authoritative voice of God.

But notice, second, that although Jesus' teaching was authoritative, *it was never in any overbearing sense didactic or dogmatic or forcing assent.* Continually, as you turn the pages of the Gospels, one fact stares out at you – the quite amazing patience of Jesus with the men he had to teach; his steadfast refusal to compel them, or dictate to them, or bend them to his will; his overwhelming respect for their personalities. Why was he so sparing with his miraculous powers? Because he had no wish to dazzle men's minds or to override their calmer judgement. Why did he take the risk, after the twelve had been only a comparatively short time with him, of sending them out to preach? Partly, at least, it was in order that they might be free to verify things for themselves; free to test, out in the whirl of life, whether what he had been giving them would really work. The keynote of all Jesus' teaching of his disciples was, 'I call you not servants, but I have called you friends' (John 15:15); and if that keynote had been remembered, his followers of a later day could never have fallen (as they have sometimes fallen) into the mistake of trying to stifle thought by loading people with infallible dogmas demanding implicit assent. 'Not slaves, but friends,' said Jesus. Not – 'There is the truth: accept it, or perish!', but 'I am the truth; live with me, and you will find it'. 'If any man will do his will, he shall know of the doctrine' (John 7:17). His teaching was authoritative always, overbearing and dogmatic never.

Closely related to this profound respect for men's personalities is a third great principle of Jesus' method: namely, *his determination to make men think for themselves.* This is a main part of every true teacher's work. If the teacher fails in this, he fails altogether. Now Jesus by his teaching gave the greatest stimulus to thought and questioning the world has ever experienced. Indeed, in one sense it would be true to say that it was far more Christ's purpose to stimulate interest than to supply answers. Notice, for instance, how often he refused to give a direct answer to a direct question. 'Who is my neighbour?' a lawyer once asked him; and the answer was, 'A certain man went down to Jericho' – that and a story (Luke 10:29ff). 'Lord, and what shall this man do?' said Peter, pointing to John. 'What is that to thee? Follow thou me' (John 21:21f). 'Lord, are there few that be saved?' asked another. 'Strive to enter in!' (Luke 13:23f). And all the parables had that for their aim – to make people use their own powers of spiritual insight and perception upon spiritual realities. 'Thou shalt love the Lord thy God,' said Jesus, quoting Deuteronomy, 'with all thy *mind*' (Mark 12:30). And again, 'He that hath ears to hear, let him hear' (Matthew 11:15 *etc*), which simply means, 'Use the spiritual powers God has given you!'

Hence we see that it was, and is, no part of the purpose of Jesus' teaching to supply ready-made answers to each and every problem of life. Problems in abundance there were and are, if he had cared to legislate on them: problems of Sabbath observance, religion and politics, master and man, and many more. But Jesus came to earth to be something better than a mechanical legislator. God was not incarnate amongst people to supply cut-and-dried solutions to all their difficulties. What the Master did aim at supplying, what he lived and died to supply, was a new and living spirit by whose light and strength people could face their problems victoriously and win their way through. As Paul puts it, 'The letter killeth, but the Spirit giveth life' (II Corinthians 3:6). And this is the liberty with which Christ makes mankind free.

A fourth great principle of Jesus' method was the fact that *what he taught, he lived*. The disciples could never feel that there was anything vague or abstract or indefinite about their Master's teaching, for it was all being made concrete and personal before their eyes, all incarnate in himself. Was it faith in God that was the lesson? How gloriously he lived that lesson out himself! Was it the forgiving of injuries he was urging upon them? How whole-heartedly he himself forgave! Was it the importance of prayer that he was teaching? He himself prayed all the night long. He did not only speak to them of the necessity of service and self-sacrifice: he took a towel, and girded himself, and washed their feet. He did not make orations about brotherhood: he went into the homes of the despised, and sat at their tables, and called them friends and brothers. Christ was the supreme Teacher, because he lived supremely what he taught, and lived it entirely non-professionally and naturally. In this he is an example for all his followers for ever. No person's religion will ever make any real impact on the world if the person is not putting himself into it, if he is not living it. But if he is, it may be irresistible anywhere.

The last great principle of Jesus' teaching to which we shall point is this – *his intimacy with and love for those he taught.* 'One loving spirit,' said St Augustine, 'sets another on fire'; and that was and is the ultimate secret of Christ's divine success as Teacher. From his loving spirit the spirits of his pupils were continually catching fire, so that the lesson, in that flame of mutual love, was no dreary discipline, but joy and romance and glory. Bungling pupils in Christ's school the disciples often were, disappointing him sorely at a score of points, stumbling sadly over his great lesson of faith and hope and love. And yet, for all the sorry show they made in these things, their love for him was growing all the time. His loving spirit was triumphing over all the hindrances in them. And a day came (it was after Calvary and Pentecost) when at long last they had their lesson – the great central message of redemption – perfect and complete and without any flaw at all; and they went forth to proclaim it to the earth.

IX
The Fatherhood of God

1 REVELATION, *not* ARGUMENT

IT is a striking fact that Jesus never argued for the existence of God. Search the Gospels from first to last for 'proofs' of God, and you will search in vain. Why?

One reason undoubtedly was this: Jesus knew that in those ultimate matters argument, taken by itself and apart from something higher, will never breed conviction. It may remove certain difficulties: it cannot beget vision. Omar Khayyam's experience is familiar:

> *Myself when young did eagerly frequent*
> *Doctor and Saint, and heard great Argument*
> *About it and about; but evermore*
> *Came out by the same Door as in I went.*

There were certain historic 'proofs' of the existence of God of which an older generation made much; but in point of fact it has never been, it is not now, and it never will be, along that road that conviction comes and people get a grip of God. A living conviction is bred by two things, each of them higher and deeper than argument: namely, the direct action of God upon the soul: which is Revelation; and the response of the soul to that divine initiative – *ie* Faith. Hence the Bible, which is psychologically as well as religiously the sanest book in the world, does not start off with – 'Let us summarise the arguments for God', or 'Now, as to the question whether there exists a God or not', or anything of the kind; but goes in one bold stride right to the heart of things with these great challenging words, like the sudden beat of a drum – *'In the beginning God.'* Hence Jesus, when he came, never stopped to prove God. He came to do something better than that. He came to reveal God.

In any case, there was no need to argue. He assumed a belief in God among his immediate hearers, and he was right to assume it. Jesus was a Jew, and his hearers were Jews, and the heart of the Jewish religion was a convinced monotheism. The essence of it was the Deuteronomic creed – 'Hear, O Israel: The Lord our God is one Lord' (Deuteronomy 6:4). The belief in God was there already, and Jesus could count on it. So much at least was common ground between the preacher and his hearers. On that basis he could go to work and build. Hence the question was not – 'Is there a God?' It was – 'Granted that there is a God, what is this God like?'

To that question Christ's answer was one constantly reiterated word – 'Father'. Within the short compass of our Gospels that name occurs more than 150 times. It is there in the first recorded boyhood utterance of Jesus – 'Wist ye not that I must be about my Father's business?' (Luke 2:49). It is there in his last dying cry – 'Father into thy hands I commend my spirit' (Luke 23:46). Christendom, with the Gospels in its hands, has inevitably fixed on this as the supreme name for God for ever.

2   *The* ORIGINAL ELEMENT *in* JESUS' TEACHING

It would not, of course, be true to suppose that Jesus was the first to call God 'Father'. Dimly and gropingly the men of the Old Testament had been feeling after this great thought on which

Christ set his seal. To begin with they conceived of God's Father-hood almost solely in the national sphere. He was the Father of the chosen people. 'Thus saith the Lord,' said Moses to Pharaoh, 'Israel is my son, even my firstborn' (Exodus 4:22). That was a national Fatherhood. But already in the Old Testament you can see men's thoughts moving out to something deeper and more personal, especially in some of the Psalms, as, for example, when God is called the 'Father of the fatherless' (68:5), or in that word of wonderful compassion and beauty – 'Like as a father pitieth his children, so the Lord pitieth them that fear him (103:13). We cannot say that Jesus was the first to call God 'Father'.

In what respects then, was his teaching here original and new? In two respects.

He took this thought that had been a stray guest, hovering uncertainly on the dim borderland and circumference of men's minds, and *made it the centre of everything.* Before Jesus, many good people had thought of God's relationship to mankind mainly in terms of a potter and his clay, or a creator and his creatures, or a dictator and his subjects. But to Jesus all these conceptions were dim half-lights, hiding as much as they revealed. The likest thing on earth to God's relationship to mankind, said Jesus, was the family relationship, the life of a father and his children. Now that new emphasis of Jesus, that centralising of this conception, was something unheard of and revolutionary; and it changed the whole face of religion.

The other respect in which Jesus' thought of God as Father was completely original was *the new depth and content he put into the word.* For not only did he make the word central: he enriched it beyond recognition. And he did that not so much by any-thing he said, as by the way he lived. Jesus, alone in history, has lived out consistently and unbrokenly and shiningly and triumphantly the kind of life that a vital sense of the divine fatherhood should imply. Here in this absolutely filial life of

Christ, this perfect sonship of the Master, all the tenderness and strength and serenity and amazing everlasting dependableness of the Father-God are mirrored. So Jesus gave the word 'Father' a depth of which mankind had never dreamed.

3 *The* MEANING *of* FATHERHOOD

Now the way is open for us to come to the heart of our subject. When Christ taught men to look up and call God 'Father', what did he mean by it? What practical consequences did he draw? (Here, for the sake of clearness, we shall set down the various truths which Jesus' thought of Fatherhood contains, giving illustrative materials from the Gospels in each case; but in the actual teaching of the subject of this lesson, it will be better to begin with the Gospel illustrations, and to lead on from these to the underlying principles.)

(1) Since God is a Father, said Jesus, *he is vitally interested in all his children's concerns.* Jesus asked the world to believe – and to believe with no 'ifs' or 'buts' or conditions, but radically and out-and-out – that even things like food and clothing are most certainly God's concern; that when 'man goeth forth unto his work, and to his labour, until the evening', God goes forth with him; and that, at the back of things, unseen and unrecognised often, but everlastingly gracious, there is a loving heart thinking for his people all the time, planning for them, remembering them, arranging wonderful surprises of sheer goodness for them. Jesus put all that into one great, simple sentence: 'If ye then' – you fathers – 'know how to give good gifts unto your children, how much more shall your Father which is in heaven give good things to them that ask him?' (Matthew 7:11).

Now Jesus did not only teach that faith. He lived it. He practised what he preached. Every page of the Gospels shows you Jesus taking the faith in a Father-God which he proclaimed to men and putting himself into it, body and soul. Out of a great mass of instances, take just one (Mark 4:37ff). There was a night on the Galilean Lake when the sudden whirlwind blew and the waves were lashed into fury, and the frail fishing-craft sagged and struggled in the trough of the waves. The fishermen looked into one another's terrified faces and cried that this was the end. But Jesus lay asleep on a pillow. To us, reading the story today, that sleeping Christ in the storm is one of the most compelling arguments for faith in the world. Asleep – why? Because it was God's sea, and the waves and the wind and the dark were in his Father's hand, and underneath were the everlasting arms.

By teaching and life, Jesus showed that to know a God who is thus vitally interested in all his children's concerns, is to have the secret of a peace, a poise and a steadiness that nothing in life can disturb. The person who has made that discovery has passed out of the bondage of fear and worry into a glorious liberty and release. He is someone who has achieved absolute independence of circumstances in utter dependence upon God; who has found what Jesus meant by 'blessedness' (Matthew 5:3ff); who is doing what the New Testament calls 'overcoming the world'. Because God is at his right hand, he shall not be moved.

(2) Since God is a Father, said Jesus, *he knows and loves each individual soul.* A father does not love his family in general: he loves each child in particular. Even so, 'the very hairs of your head are all numbered' (Matthew 10:30). 'God so loved the world' (John 3:16) is but one side of the shield: the other is this – 'There is a joy in the presence of the angels of God over *one* sinner that repenteth' (Luke 15:10). The shepherd leaves the 99 sheep in the fold, and goes out after the one (Luke 15:4-7). Christ's own redeeming work shows the individualising love of God in action. Crowds surged round Jesus, but it was the single soul that engrossed and fascinated him. There were scores of ailing folk at the Pool of Bethesda: Jesus went straight to

the one poor, desperate soul who had had 38 years of disappointment (John 5:2ff). When the slow, sad procession filed out from the gates of Nain, Jesus had eyes only for the weeping mother who had lost her boy (Luke 7:11ff). Pressed and jostled by a gaping crowd, he turned round and singled out the one shrinking soul who needed to touch him most (Mark 5:25ff). Some of the most glorious words in the Gospel were given first to one lonely woman who had bungled her life (John 4:7ff). He walked and talked with Nicodemus in the dark (John 3:1ff). He escaped from the Jericho crowd and chose Zacchaeus for his host (Luke 19:1ff). Looking at Jesus, we feel the force of St Augustine's dictum about God – 'he loves us every one as though there were but one of us to love.'

(3) Since God is a Father, said Jesus, *mankind can be absolutely natural in its religion.* By bringing in the family concept, he struck a death-blow at that devastating thing – formality in religion. People had been thinking that God could be satisfied only with pomp and ceremony (Matthew 6:5; 23:23); but that was not the way in which any earthly father wished his children to come to him, certainly God the Father of Heaven did not require it. That does not mean that we can be irreverent in our approach to God, or take liberties with him who is God over all, blessed for ever. But it does mean that the barriers of formality are down. The veil is rent in twain from top to bottom, and the way to God lies open (Matthew 27:51). One result of this is that simple petitionary prayer gains a new importance and authority. The idea that we should eliminate the element of definite petition from our prayers received no countenance from Jesus. If God is your Father, said Jesus, and you are his child, then clearly you can take all your requests and desires to him (Matthew 7:7ff). It would be unnatural to refrain from taking them, and if anything in your relationship to God is unnatural, it is wrong. By calling God 'Father', Jesus had baptised religion into a new freedom, liberty, childlike directness and simplicity.

(4) Since God is a Father, said Jesus, *pain has a meaning*. Indeed, in the old days (in many passages of the Old Testament, for instance), people were apt to think that pain, suffering, trials of all kinds, were signs of an angry God's condemnation, and judgements upon their sins. Sometimes that may be the truth, but certainly not invariably. Christ has cleared that awful thought away; and we know now that there are some kinds of suffering at least which, far from being God's condemnation of a soul, can actually be experienced – through the gracious influence of the Spirit – as God's election of that soul for signal honour. (On the other aspect of suffering as an intruder in the world, something to be challenged and removed, see the chapter on 'The Ministry of Healing'.)

So it was with Jesus himself. St Paul, describing Jesus' sufferings, says 'God spared not his own Son' (Romans 8:32). Why was he not spared? Because God had a purpose for him, a great and glorious world-redeeming purpose, and the suffering was the road to it. So God deals with all his children. 'Blessed are ye when men shall persecute you for my sake' (Matthew 5:11). As the writer to the Hebrews puts it, 'What son is he whom the father chasteneth not?' (Hebrews 12:7).

There is also another way in which the thought of God's Fatherhood lets in light on the problem of human pain. It implies that God shares in that pain himself. For if God is a Father, and you are his child, it follows that any suffering you have to face in this world is his suffering too, that anything that hurts you hurts God (because he is a real Father) far more, and that any furnace of trouble you have to pass through is seven times heated for him. 'In all their affliction, he was afflicted' (Isaiah 63:9). The supreme instance of that is Calvary. On the green hill far away they raised the Cross, but the real Cross was in heaven, in the Father-heart of the Eternal.

(5) Since God is a Father, said Jesus, *sin and forgiveness stand in a new light*. On the one hand, sin grows darker. If the power

behind the universe were sheer impersonal law, then our wrong thoughts and deeds would be sins against law. But if the power behind the universe is, as Jesus revealed, a Father, then our wrong thoughts and deeds are sins against love. And if it is bad to strike a blow at a fixed, rigid law, it is ten time worse to strike a blow at a loving heart. Indeed, to call God 'Father' is ultimately to make sin intolerable. The greatest of the parables, the story of the prodigal son (Luke 15:11ff), drives that lesson home; but not content with teaching it, Christ died to make it plain. For it was not law that men crucified on Calvary – it was God's holy love.

Crucified – but not killed! For at the Cross the Father-heart of God passed breaking-point and refused to break; and if sin stands in a new light, so does love's victory over sin, which is forgiveness. Can God forgive? – men asked before Jesus came, and the answer was always more or less in doubt. But call him Father, and at once the question becomes – How can God *not* forgive? Daringly Jesus pictured God, not waiting for his shamed child to slink home, not standing on his dignity when he came, but running out to gather him, shamed and ragged and muddied as he was, to his welcoming arms. The same name 'Father' has at once darkened the colour of sin and heightened the splendid glory of forgiveness. (This will be more fully treated in the chapter on 'Sin and its Remedy'.)

(6) Finally, since God is a Father, said Jesus, *all men are brothers.* Clearly no one has a right to take Jesus' words 'Our Father' upon his lips; no one is using the Lord's Prayer sincerely, who is not prepared to treat everyone everywhere as members of the same family as himself. In an age that is clamourous about brotherhood, it is strange surely that we do not hear more of the one great conviction on which alone a lasting brotherhood can be built – the conviction of the divine Fatherhood. (See the chapter below on 'The Royal Law of Love'.)

When Jesus implanted that conviction in men's hearts, it

was not only a law of brotherliness he was giving, but also an adequate motive. To be able to say of another person, 'That man or woman, like myself, has God for Father, he or she too is a child of God', is to be well on the way to vanquish all unbrotherly feelings. Here, at least, the dictum that 'East is East, and West is West, and never the twain shall meet' breaks down; here divergences of temperament are transcended, and jarring prejudices give way; here denominationalism falls into true perspective, and all the rifts within the lute that spoil the spiritual music are healed; here the deep cleavages of race and nationality are bridged, and at the back of the United Nations something even grander, finer, nobler begins to come into view – the Family of God. Here, in Jesus' revelation of God as Father, the hope of a unified earth has been given once and for all – the vision of the New Jerusalem coming down out of heaven, adorned as a bride for her husband.

X
Sin and its Remedy

1 JESUS *as* SAVIOUR

'THOU shalt call his name Jesus, for he shall save his people from their sins' (Matthew 1:21). 'The Son of man is come to seek and to save that which was lost' (Luke 19:10). 'This is my blood of the new testament, which is shed for many for the remission of sins' (Matthew 26:28). Sentences like these focus to a point the truth which lies on every page of the Gospels: that the coming of Christ was God's plan for the mending of a broken earth. The world to which Jesus came was sorely damaged and defaced. Wherever Jesus looked, he saw traces of the working of one disastrous power. Wherever he went, he encountered potential sons of God, whose fellowship with their Father in heaven had been destroyed by that one power. All along the line, the progress of humanity was being held up and thwarted and thrown into confusion by the one stubborn enemy – sin. Here was the ubiquitous fact with which Jesus, in seeking to establish the Kingdom, had to deal. His work on earth was the restoring of the family relationship, the fellowship of children with their Father, which sin had interrupted and over-thrown. Accordingly, our aim in the present study must be a two-fold one: first to find what Jesus had to say, by word and attitude, about sin, the disease; and then to watch his discovery and application of the remedy – namely forgiveness.

It is significant that Jesus seems to have spoken rarely of

'sin' in the singular, and nearly always of 'sins' in the plural. His interest, that is to say, was not abstract but concrete, not speculative but practical. Questions of the origin of sin, for instance, were not his primary concern; and the modern discussions of the part played in sin by the factors of environment and inheritance find but little place in the Gospels. Broken lives were never treated by Jesus as 'cases': they were brothers to be helped, and the personal interest was supreme. It was no part of Jesus' purpose to elaborate a theory of sin which would explain where it had come from, or why God should continue to tolerate it in his universe. What he attempted and gloriously carried through was something far greater than that, far more practical – the restoring of lost sons and daughters to the home in God from which their sins had shut them out.

2   *What* OUR SINS *meant to* JESUS

The Gospels make it clear that sin, to Jesus, meant anything and everything that might put a barrier between a man and his God, or between a man and his neighbour. Here Jesus' thought moved along two distinct lines.

One the one hand, *sin was the breaking of a law*. This, at first sight, might seem to be no more than the Jewish Rabbis taught; they, too, held that the law was the final standard of righteousness, and any violation of the law was sin. But in reality Jesus went much deeper than this. He was not thinking, as the Rabbis were, of any ceremonial righteousness: he was thinking of God's law written in the secret places of men's hearts. It was Jesus who first revealed the true *inwardness* of sin. This he illustrated in the Sermon on the Mount, when he showed (as against the Rabbis) that sins may be committed in thought and desire, no less than in action, and that there are sins of the mind and spirit, as well as sins of the flesh (Matthew 5:21f, 27f).

Pharisaism, which always waxed hot and indignant against sins of this latter kind, branding them as disreputable and fatal, took but little notice of such 'respectable' sins as pride and selfishness and lack of love; but it was precisely these things, these inward, spiritual sins, that called forth Christ's sternest denunciations. Bad as the sins of the flesh were, these were worse. Indeed, so strenuously did Jesus emphasise the essential inwardness of sin, that it would not be wrong to say that he regarded sin, not primarily as something that a person does, but as something a person *is*. 'Those things,' he said, 'which proceed out of the mouth come forth from the heart. Out of the heart proceed evil thoughts, murders, thefts' (Matthew 15:18f). Deep in the secret heart of man, God's eternal law stands written; and sin is in the breaking of that law.

But it is more. *It is a blow at a loving heart.* We talk about breaking a law; but that, after all, is only relatively true. In one sense, you cannot break a law: you can only be broken by it. But you *can* break a heart; and that comes nearer the truth about sin as Jesus saw it. Sin is not hurting the moral order, for an impersonal order cannot suffer. Sin is hurting love, and love can suffer dreadfully. 'O Jerusalem, Jerusalem,' cried Jesus on the Mount of Olives, 'how often would I, and ye would not!' (Matthew 23:37). The deepest shadow in the story of the prodigal is not the sufferings of the sinful son: it is the sorrow of the lonely father (Luke 15:11ff). Sin, according to Jesus, is something more than the *Shorter Catechism* has put into its definition: 'any want of conformity unto, or transgression of, the law of God'. It is something more than a blundering running of our heads against the inexorable laws of the universe. It is another nail hammered into love's cross, a clenched fist thrust up into the face of God. It is a blow struck at a loving heart.

Hence there was no minimising of our sins with Jesus. He never treated them lightly. He never excused or condoned them. Some of his contemporaries thought he did. The name 'Friend of sinners', which is today his glory, was originally flung at him as a stinging gibe by his critics: to them, his readiness to consort with sinners of all kinds seemed to argue a deficient estimate of sin, and even a flaw in his own character (Matthew 11:19). But they were forgetting, or more probably for their own ends they were deliberately ignoring, the fact that while Jesus loved all broken lives, he hated passionately the evil things that had broken them. He never spoke, like Augustine, of 'splendid sins'. Milton's Satan has a touch of glamour about him: there was no glamour in sin as Christ saw it. The idea that because God is kind and benevolent and understanding it is unnecessary to take sin too seriously, and that everything is bound to come right in the end (as in Heine's words, 'of course God will pardon me: that's his job') received no countenance from Jesus for a moment. On the contrary, we have not learned much from the Gospels if we have failed to realise that every unlovely action a person does, and every unclean thought he thinks, have Jesus Christ against them, a Christ who in his mercy has to be quite merciless to sin, whose eyes are 'as a flame of fire' (Revelation 1:14). There was no blurring of moral distinctions with Jesus. He spoke of men as 'lost' (Matthew 18:11; Luke 15:4, 8, 24) and 'perishing' (Matthew 18:14; John 3:16). In the end, he proved his implacable antagonism to sin by dying at its hands. The Cross is the measure of Jesus' view of the seriousness of sin.

3 SIN'S CONSEQUENCES

We turn next to what Jesus had to say about *the consequences of our sins*. He recognised, to begin with, that sins are often visited with *outward penalties*. The precise connection between sin and suffering is one of religion's perennial problems, and Jesus elaborated no theory about it: but he warned his hearers that God always takes men at their word, and that they must be prepared to find their sins calling forth a divine reaction. We inhabit a world made by God; it is a moral universe, and its heart is set on righteousness; and therefore we punish ourselves by our sins, as Charles Kingsley expressed it, 'just as a wheel in a piece of machinery punishes itself when it gets out of gear'. To one sufferer whom he healed, Jesus said, 'Sin no more', adding significantly, 'lest a worse thing come upon thee' (John 5:14).

But it is quite clear that in Jesus' mind any such outward penalties of human sins were dwarfed by their inward results. One such result was *the bad conscience*. 'Father,' cried the prodigal, 'I have sinned against heaven, and in thy sight, and am no more worthy to be called thy son' (Luke 15:21). It was the bad conscience that suddenly made cowards of a whole clamourous crowd when Jesus suggested that anyone among them who had no sin should cast the first stone (John 8:7); that sent Peter out into the night, weeping bitterly (Matthew 26:75); that drove Judas to his death (Matthew 27:4f).

Again, Jesus said that our sins result in *an enslaved will*. In his own declared programme, the central thing was this – 'to preach deliverance to the captives' (Luke 4:18). 'Whosoever committeth sin,' he said, 'is the servant – the bondslave – of sin' (John 8:34). He meant that wrong thoughts, once admitted to a person's heart, begin to beat a track for themselves there, to drive a thoroughfare right through his experience; and that, when that path has been made, foul shapes of sin can march up and down it at will, with none to stop them. It was the same enslaving power of sin that Marcus Aurelius was thinking of when he said, 'Whatever the mental pictures you often make, to that colour your mind comes; the mind is dyed by its pictures'. The sinner awakes one day to discover that, try as he may, he cannot forsake his sin. It has the upper-hand now. His will is enslaved.

Closely related to this is another consequence of sin which Jesus encountered – *the hardened heart*. When Jesus stood before Herod at the last, not a word would he speak (Luke 23:9 – contrast his attitude towards Pilate, John 18:33ff). That silence could only mean one thing: that the man's spiritual faculty, on the day when the Son of God confronted him, was atrophied. That is what Scripture means by the hardening of a man's heart. It is not that God predestines any soul to destruction. It is not that God shuts any one out into darkness. But a person may shut himself out. He may go on in sin until he loses the very power of recognising goodness when he sees it. It is the Nemesis of sin that it impairs the judgement and blinds the vision and hardens the heart, until even the glory of God on the face of Jesus Christ may mean just nothing. As Whittier expressed it:

> *For ever round the mercy-seat*
> *   The guiding lights of love shall burn,*
> *But what if, habit-bound, thy feet*
> *   Shall lack the will to turn?*

> *What if thine eye refuse to see,*
> *   Thine ear of Heaven's free welcome fail,*
> *And thou a willing captive be,*
> *   Thyself thy own dark jail?*

But the consequence of sin of which Jesus chiefly thought was *the loss of fellowship with God* which it involves. Supreme among all the blessings of life stood communion with the heavenly Father: hence the overwhelming gravity of sin, which always disturbs such communion. There might be love at home for the prodigal still, and an abundant welcome waiting for him when he came; but nothing could alter the fact that the lad in the far country had lost, for the time at least, his father's fellowship (Luke 15:13). It is the pure in heart who see God (Matthew 5:8); and sin, which smirches the purity, also spoils the vision. What mainly struck Jesus about the sinner's lot was its utter loneliness (Luke 15:4); and the worst element in that loneliness was not the separation of the sinner from his fellows, though that, too, was involved. It was his isolation from God.

Jesus also pointed out that one person's sins inevitably entail *consequences to others*. 'Whatsoever a man soweth, that shall he also reap' (Galatians 6:7) is not the whole truth, for others have to share the reaping. Others have to pay part of the price; and sometimes they pay in sorrow and suffering and tears, like the poor who are ruined by others' greed (Luke 20:47), or like the father whose boy goes wrong (Luke 15:11); and sometimes they even pay in sin, like God's 'little ones' to whom others play the tempter (Matthew 18:6). This is a direct outcome of what we may call the 'solidarity' of life. 'Our echoes,' says the writer Tennyson, 'roll from soul to soul.' No doubt the prodigal told himself that his way of life was his own private affair, and that if there should be a price to pay in the end for the far country's pleasures, he would have had his day and would be ready to pay up without whimpering; but he was wrong. There were others who were going to pay. Already his own father was paying. Shakespeare's Richard cries:

> *O God! if my deep prayers cannot appease Thee*
> *But Thou wilt be avenged on my misdeeds,*
> *Yet execute Thy wrath on me alone!*

That cannot be. Sin's tragedy is that it always involves others. And it was just the supreme instance of this when one day it involved God himself in a Cross.

The ultimate consequence of sin, according to Jesus, is *judgement*. Attempts are continually being made to explain away this element in Jesus' teaching, and to construct a religion with the thought of judgement left out. Such attempts will always be foredoomed to failure. The fact of judgement is rooted firmly in passage after passage of the Master's teaching (*eg* Matthew 25; Luke 12); and a religion in which this idea found no place could be constructed only at the price of mutilating the Gospels beyond recognition. Of course, we are not to interpret with a crude literalism language which Jesus always meant to be taken pictorially; but from everything he said on this great theme one fact shines out clearly: sin, if persisted in, has consequences which reach beyond this present world of time, and every one of us at the last shall give account of ourself to God.

4 SIN'S REMEDY

But Jesus came to earth not only to diagnose a malady, but also to prescribe and apply the remedy. We turn now from the disease to its cure. The remedy was forgiveness, the reconciling of sinners to God, the restoring of the lost relationship. This, of course, is something quite different from the remitting of sin's penalty, for a forgiven person may still have to bear the cost of his or her misdeeds. From the moment when Jesus said to the penitent thief, 'Today shalt thou be with me in Paradise' (Luke 23:43), the man's sin was blotted out: and yet the full penalty of death was exacted.

Still it would be wrong to suppose that forgiveness does not react even upon these outward penalties. It does. It changes them by changing the pardoned man's whole attitude to them: sometimes they even become means of grace. But, after all, the bearing of sin's continued consequences is a very small matter when it is set alongside the experience of being put right with God. And it is in this that forgiveness essentially consists.

What then did Jesus teach, by word and deed, on this great matter? In the first place, he emphasised *the glorious reality of forgiveness*. Some were slow to credit this. Things could never be the same again, they felt. Sin had cut them off too drastically. The old intimacy of fellowship could never come back. This lurking doubt was very poignantly expressed by Jesus in his greatest parable. When the lad who smirched his honour and ruined his good name came limping back, a poor shabby wreck of the life that set out from home so gaily and buoyantly not long before, he felt that he could never hope to be one of the family again – that would be too much to ask. 'I am no more worthy to be called thy son: make me as one of thy hired servants' (Luke 15:19). Men felt like debtors confronting liabilities which were utterly and for ever impossible for them to meet (Matthew 18:23ff; Luke 7:41ff). Into that feeling of hopelessness Christ broke with the glorious news of full and final restoration. Before the prodigal could get out his suggestion about the 'hired servant', his father's arms were round him (Luke 15:20). The creditor wiped the slate clean (Luke 7:42). There was no long period of probation: in a single moment, a man might leap clear from the fearful pit to the very breast of eternal love, and the most wasted, shrivelled, burned-out soul might stand erect and clean and in its right mind before God (Luke 23:43).

Another fact which Jesus made very clear was that, in restoring the lost relationship, *God holds the initiative*. It is from God's side, not the sinner's, that everything begins. Human efforts to earn and to achieve pardon are unavailing. We cannot, to use Robert Browning's words in *Johannes Agricola,* 'Make out, and reckon on, his ways, And bargain for his love, and stand, Paying a price, at his right hand'.

The Parable of the Labourers in the Vineyard settled that once and for all: in forgiveness, there is no question of merit, but all is of grace (Matthew 20:1-16). Even penitence, without which pardoning love cannot become operative, is God-created, not man-made. It is God's goodness and love, especially as these are manifested in Jesus, which evoke the penitence. So it was with Peter after his denial. 'The Lord turned, and looked upon Peter. And Peter remembered' (Luke 22:61). Then penitence came like a flood. Always God holds the initiative. It is one of the secrets of the saving power of Calvary that the sight of the

Cross can produce in a man's heart a sorrow and shame for sin which he himself could never create. Everything in the experience of being forgiven, penitence included, is the gift of God.

Notice, further, *the central place of Jesus in forgiveness*. He not only declared forgiveness – he embodied it. Sinners encountering Jesus became aware of a double effect he had upon them. On the one hand, his sinless purity searched and scorched their souls. His holiness was like a mirror in which, for the first time in their lives, they really saw themselves as they were. It happened to Peter at the beginning of his discipleship. 'Depart from me,' he cried, 'for I am a sinful man, O Lord' (Luke 5:8). It happened to the woman of Samaria. 'Come,' she exclaimed, 'see a man, which told me all things that ever I did' (John 4:29).

On the other hand, there was something in Jesus' presence that chased sinners' despair away and gave birth to great hope. When Jesus walked down the road with despised Zacchaeus at his side, he was no doubt losing for himself the respect of the crowd – but he was not thinking of that. He was restoring the man's long-vanished self-respect, and that was the first step in his salvation (Luke 19:6, 7). People felt, when they encountered Jesus, that here was one who believed in them, even when they had ceased to believe in themselves; one who was quite sure that they and he together could yet make something big and fine and clean of life: and with that, hope that had been dead came alive again, and the way for the miracle of forgiving love was open. Jesus, by his very attitude towards them, made the fact of forgiveness credible; for they felt, dimly no doubt at first, but always with growing clearness, that the love which had followed them down to the depths, and now stood by them in their shame, was the love of God himself.

The Gospels further make it clear that *Jesus connected the forgiveness of sins with his own death* (Matthew 20:28; 26:28). He knew, as we have already seen, that his death, by exposing sin in its true nature, would create penitence, and so make forgiveness possible (John 12:32). But he also knew that the same Cross which thus uncovered the sin of man, would reveal the very heart of God. Hence he was not driven to his death; it was his choice, and he went to it in the freedom of his soul. We shall have to return to the meaning of the death of Jesus at a later point in our study: suffice to say here that sinners, looking at the Cross, have always seen in it, not Jesus' love only but God's love, not merely the sacrifice of the son but the sacrifice of the father. That is what makes the love of Calvary an overpowering thing, infinitely strong to save. 'God was in Christ, reconciling the world unto himself' (II Corinthians 5:19).

Finally, Jesus spoke of *the results of forgiveness.* Two results he confidently looked for in the lives of the forgiven. He looked for *love.* And he was never disappointed: love always came. The breaking of the alabaster box, as Jesus pointed out to Simon the Pharisee, was a symbol of the newborn love which the experience of a great pardon had created (Luke 7:37ff). And he looked for *goodness.* He expected forgiveness to be a regenerative force, re-making character. Here again his hopes were realised. Zacchaeus, having been saved, immediately and of his own accord, faced up to the moral issues of salvation: he announced his purpose of restitution (Luke 19:8). What made Peter the mighty apostle that he became was the discovery that Jesus forgave him for the hour of black shame in the high priest's courtyard, and was willing, with the gracious words 'Feed my sheep', to trust him all over again; that made him a man of God indeed (John 21:15ff). No one who reads the Gospels will ever be led astray by the argument that to pardon freely is simply to condone sin, and therefore to make for the demoralisation of the sinner. To know oneself forgiven – and forgiven at so great a cost – is always a moral dynamic of the first order. It is a mainspring of the dedicated life. It creates character. It works righteousness. It brings honour back to the throne. It makes the forgiven sinner Christ's person, body and soul, for ever.

XI
The Ministry of Healing

1 *The* GOOD PHYSICIAN

THERE are two ways of approaching this subject. We can single out from the Gospel story one typical instance where Christ wrought a cure, and try to probe its methods and meaning; or we can take the Gospel picture as a whole, and let that speak to us of his healing work. Here we shall take the second way.

The ministry of healing was an integral part of the work Christ came into the world to do. It was an essential element of his mission and vocation. It was not a side issue: it was a function which Jesus himself invariably ranked along with his teaching and preaching. The healing miracles were no mere incidental works of pity, but the fruit of Jesus' strong conviction that he had come into the world to redeem our human personality in all its aspects – physical as well as spiritual – and to offer unto God his Father whole individuals. And indeed we can see that if he was to be Redeemer at all, he was bound to take that line. Soul and body are inextricably welded together, and are continually acting and reacting on each other. Hence the ministry of healing was an integral part of Christ's God-given task. He recognised it as that himself: for when he sent his followers out to carry on his work, it was with a dual commission that he sent them – to preach and to heal (Mark 3:15; Luke 10:9).

Accordingly, any efforts to eliminate this side of things from the story, to draw Christ as the winsome teacher and persuasive preacher and nothing more, to construct a Gospel with these mighty works of healing, and indeed everything that is commonly ranked under the name 'miracle', left out – any such efforts are foredoomed to failure. No doubt there will always be some who declare that if these things were away, a stumbling-block to faith would be removed. Some there may be who would almost prefer Jesus the simple teacher. But one thing is certain – eliminate the supernatural from your thoughts of Jesus, and you may still have something that you find valuable left: you have certainly not the Christ of the Gospels left, but a different being altogether. Beyond all question, the mighty works of Jesus are part of the very texture of the evangelical record, and a main part of our Lord's mission to the earth.

2 *The* COMPASSION *of* CHRIST

The fact, then, of the healing ministry of Jesus is fixed and clear. What we have to do now is to try to interpret that fact. We have to explore its Why and its How. In other words, two questions confront us: one a question of Motive, the other a question of Method. Why did Jesus devote himself to the curing of disease? And how were his cures wrought?

Take first the question of Motive. According to one view, the answer is simple: Jesus did his mighty works deliberately to draw attention to himself, proving his divinity, and thus enforcing his teaching. It was necessary (this view holds) for Jesus to draw attention to himself, and these dramatic works were his chosen way of doing it. They were the trumpet Jesus sounded to attract the world's notice. They were the credentials Jesus offered the world in proof of his claims. They were the testimonials of the Master's divinity. Their motive was self-authentication. They were there to create belief in Christ.

It needs only a little thought to show how wide of the mark

this view is. For one thing, it directly contradicts the evidence of the Gospels themselves. It says that Jesus did his mighty works in order to draw attention to himself and broadcast his claims. Is that what the Gospels say? On the contrary, the Gospels give us a Christ who fled from fame. The Gospels give us a Christ who again and again followed up his cures with an immediate injunction to secrecy. 'See thou tell no man!' (Matthew 8:4; Mark 8:26; Luke 8:56). Does that look like broadcasting his claims? And why was Jesus so emphatic about secrecy, so determined not to make miracles a kind of public testimonial to himself? Because the whole idea of appealing to people by miracles, the whole method of driving people into belief in themselves by startling, dramatic deeds, was foreign to his nature. Out in the desert of the Temptation, he renounced once and for all the chance of getting on to the throne of the world by the miraculous. That is what his refusal of the suggestion to throw himself down from the pinnacle of the Temple meant. If he was to win the hearts of mankind at all, it was to be not by startling miracle, but by simple holiness and suffering love. Whatever the motive of the healing ministry may have been, it was not to accredit himself.

Moreover, if Jesus' motive for his mighty works had been to prove his divinity, surely he would have kept the power of doing such works to himself. But what we find in the Gospels is the reverse. Jesus believed that ordinary people could share that power. Indeed, he deliberately transmitted his own power to others. Quite certainly he meant his first disciples to exercise it too. And quite certainly they did, in some degree, exercise it. Hence his ruling motive cannot have been to raise himself to lonely divine grandeur.

In any case, such a motive would have failed in its effect: miracles do not, and never will, create belief – not real saving belief at any rate. And Jesus knew that perfectly. 'If they hear not Moses and the prophets,' he said, 'neither will they be persuaded, though one rose from the dead' (Luke 16:31): a statement which was amply verified when Christ himself rose from the dead. That is not how Christian conviction comes. To begin with miracles, and argue from them up to Christ, is beginning at the wrong end. And in point of fact, that is not how we became believers. It was not by accepting the miracles that we grew convinced of Christ. It was because we had already grown convinced of Christ, along other lines, that we can accept the miracles – a very different thing. Let us keep our perspective right. The mighty works of Jesus must have had some other deeper motive than a mere demonstration and proof of power.

According to the Gospels, there were two motives. On the one hand, there was *Christ's compassion for all hurt things.* When Jesus laid his hands upon a leper's sores, it was not with an eye to effect, any more than his taking the children into his arms had an eye to the effect on the spectators. Any such idea of Jesus trying to produce a favourable impression is horrible. It would give us an unnatural Christ. No, Jesus carried the lambs in his bosom because he loved them – just that; and Jesus touched the leper's sores because he pitied him with all his heart. The ruling motive of the mighty works of Jesus was always and everywhere compassion.

And it was not a cheap compassion. The word 'compassion' is a compound of two Latin words, and means 'suffering with'. That is what it meant for Jesus – suffering with the leper, suffering with the epileptic, suffering with the anxious father, suffering with the broken-hearted mother. So absolute was his self-identification with his brothers and sisters of the earth, that every wound of theirs was his wound too, every pain his pain, every sorrow his sorrow. Roman Catholics sometimes speak of 'the five wounds of Jesus', meaning the four nail-prints and the spear thrust. Five wounds? The heart of Jesus carried a thousand wounds. 'Himself,' said Matthew, quoting Isaiah, for he had seen at close quarters what this redeeming compassion was costing his Master, 'Himself took our infirmities, and bare our sicknesses' (Matthew 8:17; Isaiah 53:4). And often the compassion that healed was an agony.

The other motive of Christ's mighty works which the Gospels suggest is this: *in God's world Jesus always regarded disease as an intruder.* It was not part of the plan, not directly devised by God's goodwill. It was not native to God's kingdom. It was alien. Therefore Jesus, whenever he met it, set himself to destroy it.

This aspect has not been adequately emphasised. There was no false resignation about Jesus. Never was a sufferer turned away with, 'I am sorry, friend, but I cannot heal you, because God wants you to suffer'. Jesus was not resigned to leprosy or the sobs of little children. Where this whole darker side of human life is concerned, Christ was never a model of acquiescence. Christ was first and last a fighter. No doubt in a sense it is a true philosophy which says, 'God's in his heaven, all's right with the world'. But it is a deeper, truer philosophy which says that Christ is God come out of his heaven because things were wrong with the world; God come forth to challenge the alien, intruding things, and to put a wrong world right.

In this connection it is interesting to notice that Jesus often used the work of healing, both his own and his followers' work, to illustrate the break-up of the kingdom of Satan. Remember that in Jesus' day diseases were regularly attributed to demonic agency, not only cases of 'possession' (which were most obviously attributable to evil spirits), but all kinds of sickness. The unseen world was held to be full of these malign influences, emissaries of the Evil One. Hence, whenever a cure was wrought, it meant that one of these spirits had been cast out. And therefore when, through Jesus and his followers, the work of healing suddenly began to go forward on a gigantic scale, it meant that the whole kingdom of evil and darkness and Satan was being shaken to its foundations, was indeed breaking up, and the kingdom of goodness and light and God was at last coming into its own. 'If I with the finger of God cast out devils,' said Jesus, 'no doubt the kingdom of God is come upon you' (Luke 11:20). And when his seventy followers came back with the news of marvellous cures, Jesus rejoiced in spirit and cried, 'I beheld Satan as lightning fall from heaven' (Luke 10:18). Hence the miracles, which were primarily works of divine compassion, were also illustrations of the great central theme of the Master's teaching: that the Kingdom of God was at hand.

3 *The* POWER *of* GOD *in* JESUS

Up to this point, we have been considering the question of Motive, the Why of Jesus' healing ministry. Now we look at the How: the question of Method. *How were his cures wrought?* Right in the forefront of our answer, one fact must stand – *the sinlessness of Jesus, his moral perfection.* The mighty works of Jesus, it must be stressed, were in no sense a magical achievement: they were, through and through, a moral achievement.

We are apt to lay down the law as to what is possible, and what is not possible, in this world. But does not that, for beings like ourselves whose own nature has never quite escaped the thraldom and inevitable limitation that sin imposes, savour of unwarranted presumption? Suppose that one day there were to appear a being who, unlike ourselves, had escaped that thraldom and those limitations and was absolutely and finally pure and sinless, then obviously you would have a new, unprecedented, incalculable factor upon the scene; and perhaps that incalculable purity might also liberate incalculable energies?

'My strength is as the strength of ten, Because my heart is pure,' sings the poet. If, then, strength of personality varies in direct proportion to purity of life (there is evidence to show that in a very real sense it does), then absolute purity might well be matched with absolute strength of saving personality.

Now, the point is that that sinless being has appeared. In Jesus of Nazareth, the unprecedented factor has arrived. Hence the mighty works of Jesus are not in any way surprising. The surprise would have been if he had *not* done them. They were the normal expression of his personality, the outflow of his moral uniqueness. And the supreme instance of this was the Resurrection. To the men of the early days who had felt at first-hand the impact of the sinless personality of Jesus, the Resurrection was never a problem. They knew that, in his moral perfection, he was a conquering soul: therefore disease and death had to submit (note specially Acts 2:24). Let it be emphasised again – at the back of all Jesus' mighty works was that one unprecedented factor, a sinless personality. Perhaps if we were more like Jesus, the works that he did we should do also.

Alongside the sinlessness of Jesus stands another factor in his healing power – *his mighty faith in God.* 'Why could not we cast him out?' said the disciples to Jesus, when they had been trying to work a cure in a case of demon-possession and had lamentably failed. Straight as an arrow to its mark came the answer: 'Because of your unbelief' (Matthew 17:20). And Christ faced that same desperate case, and in a moment the cure had happened. They had tried to do it, half-doubting and wondering whether God's power could possibly get through here; and that half-doubt had blocked the channel completely, and God's power could not get through. Jesus had tried it, absolutely confident that God's power could get through here or anywhere; and that confidence had flung wide the gates, and the power streamed through. 'Whatever ye shall ask, believing,' said Jesus, 'ye shall receive' (Matthew 21:22); his own life was one long, stupendous application of that principle. The mighty works of Jesus were the Father's answers to the faith of the Son.

But more than Jesus' sinlessness and faith in God entered into the miracles. *People's faith in Jesus, and through Jesus in God,* was also involved. There were times when Jesus found his passion to heal balked, places where the Son of God's shadow fell and nothing happened: the sick were sick still, the maimed still maimed. Why? Because they were not expecting anything to happen. Nazareth was one of the places where that spirit thwarted love. 'Jesus?' they said incredulously. 'Why, he is one of ourselves: nothing to be looked for from him!' In that atmosphere, says the Evangelist, Christ could not even begin to work (Matthew 13:58). Sometimes, too, where a rudimentary faith did exist, it was just a spark, and before anything could happen it had to be fanned into a flame. That was why Jesus sometimes spoke to his patient for a time before any healing word was given. That, too, is doubtless why he touched the maimed and wounded places (Mark 7:33). It was to elicit faith, to crystallise the patient's vague hopes into real expectancy. Then the cure came – not before. What Jesus loved more than anything was to find someone who had daring enough to pitch his demands high and to be so sure that he was right to do it that he would simply take no denial (Mark 10:46ff). Give me faith like that, said Jesus, and all things will be possible!

But when all is said, the healing ministry of Jesus runs back to this: that *in him the power of God was present in the earth,* and present in an absolutely unimpeded form at last. Everything turns on that. This was nothing less than the Spirit of God, the living God, in action. To the disciples, as they came to share something of that Spirit, something of the same power was given. But in the great words of the Fourth Gospel – 'God gives him the Spirit in no sparing measure' (John 3:34, Moffatt). The story of Jesus, who went about continually doing good to mankind, is the story of immeasurable energy in contact with measurable need. Here the eternal love of heaven was meeting the transient tragedies of earth. Nothing else could have happened on the battlefield but what did happen: need and tragedy had to own themselves defeated, and love and life were victors. For the work of Jesus was the work of the everlasting God.

XII
The Prayer Life of Jesus

1 TEACH US *to* PRAY

A SENTENCE of Luke's gives us our starting-point: 'It came to pass that, as he was praying in a certain place, when he ceased, one of his disciples said unto him, Lord, teach us to pray' (Luke 11:1). We are not to suppose, of course, that before this the disciples had never prayed, and that now they were just beginning. Probably all of them, or nearly all, were already men of prayer. Reared in devout and simple homes, Peter and Andrew and James and John had no doubt learned to say their prayers at their mothers' knees. But note the particular circumstances of this request which St Luke records. It was when Jesus had been praying with them, and the prayer was just finished, that the request was made. No doubt often before this they had felt the difference between Jesus' prayers and their own: his so sure, strong and real, theirs so weak, stammering and intermittent; his so comprehensive, God-inspired and prevailing, theirs so erratic, spasmodic and unsatisfying. But today that difference had come home to them with a rush of overwhelming awe, and they suddenly felt that if this was prayer, they had still to learn the very rudiments of it. 'Lord,' they said beseechingly, after that evening's worship, 'Lord, teach us to pray.'

Two preliminary points are noteworthy. One is the striking fact that *Jesus never argued for the validity of prayer any more than he argued for the existence of God*. God was not something to be proved by argument: God was simply there, the beginning and the end of experience. Just so, prayer was not something to be proved by argument: prayer was there, the native breath of the soul. Prayer was mankind's instinctive tendency, wrought into the very constitution of his nature. Its well-springs lay deep down beneath the region of argument: they lay in hearts which God had made for fellowship with himself, which therefore (as St Augustine at a later day expressed it) would always be restless until they found their rest in him. Hence Jesus never argued the matter. But certainly there was a sense in which his own prayer life was the one unanswerable argument. Did any disciple – Thomas, for example – have doubts about prayer, genuine, honest doubts? Nothing was more likely to vanquish his doubts than the sight of Jesus upon his knees. For knowing Jesus, and realising what an utterly sure and reliable insight Jesus had into all the deepest things of life, such a disciple would feel it better to trust Jesus' certainty rather than his own uncertainty. He would think it wise to attach more importance to Christ's conviction than to his own doubts. In all matters of faith this is an enormously valuable principle; and certainly it carries weight here. Doubts are dispelled and dissolved before the shining prayer life of the Christ. The praying Christ is the supreme argument for prayer.

The other preliminary point to be noticed is this: that when the disciples went to school with Jesus in this matter of prayer, there were really two departments in the curriculum – *the precepts of Jesus, and the practice of Jesus.* On the one hand, there were the things the Master said about prayer, his deliberate lessons on the subject; on the other hand, there was his own life of communion with God. Now, it is not really possible to keep these two aspects separate. At every point they meet and mingle. Christ's teaching about prayer was the fruit of his own secret life of prayer: and his life of prayer was simply his teaching in action. Hence we shall draw upon them both equally and indiscriminately in our study here. There are three great facts which claim our attention. First, prayer was the habitual atmosphere of Jesus' daily life. Second, Jesus was found praying at all the great crises of his career. Third, our Lord's prayers contained many different elements, petition as well as communion, intercession no less than thanksgiving.

2 *The* PRACTICE *of the* PRESENCE *of* GOD

Prayer was the habitual atmosphere of Jesus' daily life. Evidence of this can be found on almost every page of the Gospels. We see Jesus rising up in the early morning to pray, while all the world was still asleep, 'a great while before day,' says St Mark (1:35); Jesus, after a day of incessant toil that might well have worn his spirit out, keeping his watch with God all through the night (Mark 6:46); Jesus, when the crowds surged round him and broke in upon his privacy and clamoured greedily for his help, sending his heart and thoughts heavenward to clutch for a moment at his Father's hand (Mark 7:34). It is there on page after page of the Gospels. And when, to all that, there is added this fact – that by far the largest part of Jesus' prayer life must have been secret, beyond the observation of the Twelve and even of Peter, James and John, the most intimate three, and therefore unrecorded in any of the Gospels – we begin to realise that prayer was not only an important part of his life: it *was* his life, the very breath of his being.

This means that none of the things which commonly thwart and stifle our human prayers had any power at all with Christ.

Thus, for example, his prayer life was never at the mercy of *moods*. Changes of feeling Jesus certainly knew. He was no passionless Stoic. He knew joy and sorrow, smiles and tears, ecstasy and weariness. But through it all, his heart turned to prayer, like the compass to the north. Prayer meant communing with the one he loved best in heaven and earth. Jesus loved God his Father so utterly and so passionately that he could not bear to be away from him, but used every opportunity the days and nights brought him to go and speak to the God of his love again. This means that those failures in our own prayer life, traceable back to lack of mood, are really, according to Jesus, a symptom of something deeper: they are a symptom of a breakdown of affection. Christ bids us go and give God our love.

Another thing which commonly stifles prayer is our *busy-ness*. The days are so full that prayer gets crowded out. Sometimes when that happens the plea is urged in extenuation that work itself is prayer, that honest work is one of the highest kinds of prayer which can ever be offered: therefore, the crowding out of the devotional hour does not really matter very much.

But look at Jesus. Busy and crowded as our days are, his were emphatically more so. Read the opening chapters of St Mark's Gospel. There you have a number of pictures of typical days in Jesus' ministry, days that were quite usual and normal for Jesus; and as you study these pictures and see how one duty was heaped upon another, how sick people and broken sinners came clamouring for him until far into the night and none of them were sent away unhelped, you can almost see the virtue going out of him and can realise something of the strain and the drain of it; and yet the harder the days were, the more time Jesus made for prayer. There was a whole world to be redeemed, and he alone was to be Redeemer. There was a thoroughgoing revolution in mankind's thinking and morals to be achieved, and he had only his own body and soul as instruments of that revolution. Yet the world's greatest toiler was also the world's most shining example of the daily, hourly practice of the presence of God. And as for the plea, true no doubt up to a point, that work itself is prayer, never for a moment would Jesus countenance it when it made work a substitute for prayer. The whole force of Christ's precept and practice was this: that there could be *no* substitute for prayer. However busy a person's life, he must, he can, make time to shut the door and kneel.

Another thing which often thwarts prayer is *impatience*. People think the door ought to open at their first knock; when it does not, they give up knocking and turn away. How different it was with Jesus! The writer to the Hebrews in one place speaks of Jesus offering up 'prayers and supplications, with strong crying and tears, unto him that was able to save him' (5:7); and whatever else that may mean, it certainly means this: that prayer for Jesus was a strenuous, serious business, involving every energy of mind and heart and soul. It is the same truth that shines out of the great parable of the man who knocked at his neighbour's door at midnight (Luke 11:5ff). 'Shameless' (verse 8), Jesus calls him, and then blesses him for his shamelessness! 'That is the very spirit of prayer,' he says in effect. 'Take no denial! Knock again! Beat at heaven's gate!'

Of course, Jesus never meant to imply that God was unwilling to give, or churlish to his children's cry; but he did mean that half-hearted praying was worse than useless, and that often it is only when a man's importunity has given proof of his earnestness that God's answer can come. That was the reason why Jesus always had a special love for people who came to him and would simply take no denial – the Syrophoenician woman who refused to go away (Mark 7:25ff); blind Bartimaeus at the roadside, whose 'Son of David, have mercy' no threats or entreaties could silence (Mark 10:46ff); the men who, finding the door blocked, broke up the roof rather than go away disappointed (Mark 2:4ff). If Jesus had a special love for these, it was because he felt that here was the very spirit that would prevail with God; here was real prayer in action. So people's impatience in prayer stands rebuked.

Finally, there are moral difficulties that sometimes impede our human prayers. Communion with God inevitably grows feeble and unreal if, in our own lives, there is some moral decision which we are not prepared to face. A background of absolute moral honesty is the first essential of prayer. Only the pure in heart, said Jesus, can see God. Electricians speak of insulators', meaning that these automatically break the contact and cut off the current. Sin is an insulator that breaks our prayer contact with God. 'If I regard iniquity in my heart,' said the Psalmist, 'the Lord will not hear me' (Psalm 66:18). This is the root of most of our troubles with prayer. But clearly this never laid an inhibiting hand upon the prayers of Jesus. Tempted in all points like ourselves, he kept his soul free from the faintest shadow of sin. Purity of heart sees God, and Christ's matchless purity saw God continually. Nothing was allowed to break the contact of the Son with the Father.

We see, then, that the things which commonly thwart and stifle our human prayers had no power with Christ. Prayer was the habitual atmosphere of his daily life. That is our first great fact. We turn now to the second.

3 PRAYER *and* CRISIS

Jesus was found praying at all the great crises of his career. There was a day when his call came, a sudden, swift summons to his life-work. 'It came to pass,' says Luke, 'that Jesus being baptised, and praying, the heaven was opened, and the Holy Ghost descended' (Luke 3:21). There you have Jesus praying *about his vocation.* There was a day when the first apostolic band had to be chosen, and the momentous decision made about the right men for carrying on his work. St Luke, describing the night before the decision, says, 'He went out into a mountain to pray, and continued all night in prayer to God' (Luke 6:12). There you have Jesus praying *for guidance.* There was a day when all the Twelve had been baffled by a peculiarly difficult case of demon-possession which seemed quite incurable, and only when they had given it up as hopeless, and referred it to Jesus, was heal-ing wrought and the evil spirit cast out. 'Why could not we cast him out?' they asked Jesus later. And the answer was – 'This kind can come forth by nothing but by prayer' (Mark 9:29). There you have Jesus praying *for strength for his mighty works*. There was a day when Gethsemane closed round him, and the hour and power of darkness had come, and the temp-tation to desert God's high road grew fierce. 'Being in an agony,' says the Evangelist, 'he prayed' (Luke 22:44). There you have Jesus praying *against temptation*. And finally there was an hour when the nails and torture of Calvary had almost finished their work, and strength was ebbing away, and Jordan rolled its waters at his feet. 'Father,' cried Jesus, 'into thy hands I commend my spirit' (Luke 23:46). There you have the Jesus who *died praying*. So, at all the great crises of his career, and even in the moment of death, Christ was found in prayer.

Now there, too, he was a pattern to his first followers, and to all other followers for ever. For crises such as these, through which Christ prayed his way, come to all of us. The true disciple, like his Master, will be found praying at the opening of his life-work, praying for guidance in all life's momentous decisions, praying for strength to do the works of God, praying for victory when temptation assaults, praying when on his day of life the night is falling. Every hour of crisis will find him, as it found Jesus, deep in prayer.

4 FACTORS *in* PRAYER

We turn finally to the third great fact which emerges from the Gospel picture of the prayer life of Jesus: *the prayers of our Lord had many different elements in them – Communion, Thanksgiving, Petition, Intercession.*

Communion – for often Jesus would turn to God, not for the sake of any gift that he required, but simply for the sake of God's own fellowship. 'As he prayed,' says Luke, describing one such occasion, 'the fashion of his countenance was altered' (Luke 9:29). That was the prayer of communion, when heart spoke to heart, the Spirit of Jesus on the mountain to the Spirit of his Father in heaven; and so deep and rich and precious was that hour of utter intimacy that Jesus, as the Evangelist says, came out of it with the glow and wonder written on his very face, making it radiant like an angel's. The prayer life of Jesus warns us against the view that would make prayer a mere asking of things from God. We do not make our human friendships mere matters of convenience, approaching a friend only when we desire a favour, and never going near at any other time. No friendship could survive long on these mercenary terms. And Jesus would have us reflect that least of all can our friendship with God survive on such a basis. Jesus would have us go to God when there is nothing to ask, go to him not for his gifts, but for himself alone. That is the prayer of communion – and when a human heart goes out Godward in this way, God comes to meet it, and it experiences the blessed invasion of God's presence. In such an experience, a person's whole life, like the face of Christ who prayed on the Mount of Transfiguration, is changed, for it comes to bear something of the afterglow of heaven.

Thanksgiving was another element in Christ's prayers. It was often praise and gratitude that drove him to his knees. Never did there creep into his prayers that note of aggrieved, protesting querulousness which sometimes marks our own. Always it was this amazing goodness of God his Father that filled and flooded his soul. And it was not only life's sunshine splendours that brought the cry of thanksgiving to his lips: the darkness found his gratitude unquenched. He took the broken bread, symbol of his broken body, and gave God thanks (Luke 22:19). He took the cup, seeing his own blood in it, and gave God thanks (Luke 22:17). He went out from the upper room to the sweat and agony of Gethsemane, singing a hymn, and giving God thanks (Mark 14:26). In the darkness as in the light, praise was the dominant note of Jesus' prayers; and even the Cross itself could not silence it.

Another element in Jesus' prayers was *Petition.* We have seen already that asking for God's gifts was certainly not the whole or even the main part of the Master's prayer life; but we must be careful not to go to the other extreme and imagine that such petitionary prayers found no place at all. It is particularly necessary at the present time to emphasise this, for there is a dangerous tendency today, even among good Christian people, to speak disparagingly of petitionary prayers, and to say that asking for definite things from God is prayer of such a rudimentary and childish form that it ought to have no place in the religion of the mature and fully developed believer. This we must deny. The idea that it is expedient to outgrow petitionary prayer goes to pieces on one fact: Jesus never outgrew it. On the contrary, he deliberately encouraged it and urged men to use it. He settled that once and for all in the first two words of the great prayer he taught his disciples: 'When ye pray, say, Our Father' (Luke 11:2). For if God is really your Father, and if you are really his child, it cannot be wrong to bring him definite requests and petitions: indeed, it would be unnatural *not* to. Such petitions, of course, must always be subject, in our case as in Christ's, to the great ruling condition – 'Thy will be done' (Matthew 26:39, 42); for God's wisdom may have to refuse what our heart craves. But our point is this: that the tendency to disparage petitionary prayer argues chiefly a lack of faith. Down at its roots there is lurking the thought that God is not fully at liberty, but in some sense bound, in some degree a prisoner in his universe. What Christ would have us realise is that God is alive and God is free: true faith will always do as Jesus himself did, and carry its requests straight to the throne.

Finally, Jesus' prayers contained much *Intercession.* He prayed for the little children (Mark 10:16). He prayed on the Cross for his enemies (Luke 23:34). He prayed for his disciples (John 17:9). He prayed for Judas. How terribly he wrestled in prayer for the soul of Judas only God and Jesus knew. One day when alone with his disciples, he exclaimed, 'Simon, Simon, behold Satan hath desired to have you, that he may sift you as wheat: but I have prayed for thee, that thy faith fail not' (Luke 22:31f); and we cannot but feel that it must have meant something mighty to Peter to know that the everlasting arms of that intercession were underneath him, bearing him up.

Then though our foul and limitless transgression
  Grows with our growing, with our breath began,
Raise Thou the arms of endless intercession,
  Jesus, divinest when Thou most art man!

And to every disciple that same priestly ministry of intercession has, under Jesus, been committed.

The practical conclusion to which our study of the prayer life of Jesus, as revealed in the Gospels, leads, is that prayer must ever be the heart and centre of all true religion, and the dynamic and driving power of all the best and noblest living. When John Bunyan's pilgrims were passing through the Enchanted Ground, they saw 'a man upon his knees, with hands and eyes lifted up, and speaking, as they thought, earnestly to one that was above. They drew nigh, but could not tell what he said; so they went softly till he had done. When he had done he got up, and began to run towards the Celestial City'. It is those who are often, like Mr Standfast, upon their knees, speaking earnestly to One above, who are able to march and run where others only halt and stumble. It is those who have learned the way of prayer from Jesus who have found the secret of victorious life. They go from strength to strength; every one of them appeareth before God in Zion.

XIII
The Great Confession

1 *The* TURNING-POINT

THE day at Caesarea Philippi marks the watershed of the Gospels. From this point onwards, the streams begin to flow in another direction. The current of popularity which seemed likely in the earlier days of Jesus' ministry to carry him to a throne, has now been left behind. The tide sets towards the Cross. The Galilean sunshine is suddenly clouded over, and the air grows sultry and heavy with the gathering storm. The voices shouting applause die away, and another more ominous note is heard. At Caesarea Jesus stood, as it were, on a dividing-line. It was like a hilltop from which he could see behind him all the road he had travelled, and in front of him the dark, forbidding way awaiting him. He cast one look back to where the after-glow of happy days still lingered, and then faced round and marched forward towards the shadows. His course was now set for Calvary.

Caesarea Philippi lay in the far north, where the springs of Jordan took their rise near the base of Mount Hermon. Alone with his disciples in this secluded region, Jesus brought them face to face at last with the most momentous question of their lives: 'Whom say ye that I am?' (Matthew 16:13ff; Mark 8:27ff; Luke 9:18ff).

2 *The* RESERVE *of the* MESSIAH

Now here it is necessary to remind ourselves that, whatever views and verdicts the disciples or the outside world may have formed about the position and personality of Jesus, his own mind, from the very opening of his ministry, was never visited by any shadow of doubt. He knew himself to be Messiah. And (this goes even deeper) he knew himself to be, in a unique and lonely sense, Son of God. It was that knowledge, as we have seen, which lay behind his three great original temptations: apart from it, the wilderness scene would be quite inexplicable. Certainly it was present at his baptism in Jordan. It is some-times suggested that it was at the baptism that the awareness of Messiahship and Sonship first dawned on Jesus' soul; but sure-ly it is far more probable that all through the silent Nazareth years the conviction was gradually taking shape, and that what happened in the hour of baptism was not a sudden awakening of Jesus to his own nature and function, but the receiving of power from on high, the setting of a seal by God upon the gradual discovery of years. In any case, it is clear that there never was a time in Jesus' ministry when he did not know him-self with utter certainty to be Messiah and Son of God.

But until this day at Caesarea, that knowledge had been largely veiled. A certain reserve and reticence had characterised it. Jesus, knowing himself Messiah, did not proclaim it from the house-tops. The sick people whom he healed were forbidden to publish the matter (Matthew 8:4; 9:30; Mark 5:43). The evil spirits who, feeling his power, guessed at his identity and shouted it aloud, were condemned to silence (Mark 1:24). When John the Baptist from his prison put the question directly, 'Art thou he that should come?', Jesus pointed away from himself to his works, adding significantly, 'Blessed is he, whosoever shall not be offended in me': an answer which, while sufficiently revealing the truth to John, would not disclose it to

others (Matthew 11:2ff). With the same end in view, he deliberately chose as his favourite title the enigmatic 'Son of Man'.
This name had associations (notably Daniel 7:13) which to the
spiritually-minded, and to them alone, would give a hint of
Jesus' Messianic dignity: to others it would convey nothing.
Only those who had 'ears to hear' would understand. Even on
the day of Caesarea Philippi itself, when the truth stood fully
revealed, Jesus 'charged his disciples that they should tell no
man that he was the Christ' (Matthew 16:20). As one of our
Scripture paraphrases puts it:

> *His greatness he for us abased,*
> *For us his glory veiled;*
> *In human likeness dwelt on earth,*
> *His majesty concealed.*

Why did Jesus practise this reserve? Not because his own
mind was troubled with doubts: that answer, as we have just
seen, is ruled out. There seem to have been two reasons.

On the one hand, the Messiah of whom the Jews for centuries had been dreaming, was a very different being from the
Messiah whom God was now sending to them. The popular
expectation was full of political and nationalist elements. The
Messiah, when he came, would lift his nation from the dust.
He would forcibly restore the throne of David. He would break
the heathen with a rod of iron. These were the hopes smoul-
dering in men's hearts, and it needed only the appearance of a
Messianic claimant to fan the glowing embers to a flame. It
had happened in the past when false Messiahs had arisen, and
it would assuredly have happened again if Jesus had chosen to
press his claims from the outset. The danger that the people
'would come and take him by force, to make him a King' (John
6:15) – a King, that is, after their own national and mundane
desires – was never far away. Hence before Jesus could publicly

proclaim himself Messiah, he had to transform and spiritualise the whole conception. He had to set it free from the political accretions of centuries. In particular, he had to find a place in it for the fact of suffering; the idea of a suffering Messiah was utterly foreign to his contemporaries' thoughts. Here, then, we have one reason for Jesus' reserve. His first aim, he saw, must be to arouse mankind spiritually; until that was done, the proclamation of Messiahship could only create misconception and stimulate earthly, passionate hopes of a kind with which he was totally out of sympathy; hopes which, therefore, could never be fulfilled.

The other reason for Jesus' reticence (concerning his Sonship even more than his Messiahship) lay in the fact that the greatest truths can only be revealed, not by words and proclamations, but by life and love. One day when Jesus was walking in Solomon's porch in the Temple, some of his fellow-countrymen accosted him: 'How long dost thou make us to doubt? ... If thou be the Christ, tell us plainly' (John 10:24). But the greatest things in life cannot be 'told' in that way. Can you 'tell plainly' what honour is, or beauty, or love? Can you put a sunset into a sentence? Can you express the glory and mystery and magic of a great symphony in one terse phrase? None of life's really moving experiences or discoveries can be told plainly in words. So how can we expect the greatest and most moving of all to be thus told: the glory of God on the face of Jesus Christ? Jesus knew that it would not be by any voice proclaiming 'I am the Son of God' that this conviction would be born in human hearts. But the wind bloweth where it listeth; and the men who live with him and love him learn his nature and his name.

3 *The* GREATEST QUESTION *in the* WORLD

On that day at Caesarea Philippi, when the crowds had been left behind and he was alone with the Twelve, Jesus felt that all need for reserve was gone. Quite suddenly he put to them the most momentous question with which any soul can ever be faced, 'Whom say ye that I am?'

How all-important this question is, and how deep its practical issues for life, may be illustrated by the familiar story of Thomas Carlyle. On a day when death had darkened his home, and his heart was sore, someone read to him the great words, 'Let not your heart be troubled. In my Father's house are many mansions' (John 14:1ff). 'Aye,' broke out the bereaved man, 'if you were God, you had a right to say that; but if you were only a man, what do you know any more than the rest of us?' Until then, he had been inclined to regard the question about the divine-human nature of Jesus as a vague, remote, unpractical thing; but now suddenly, under the pressure of life, he had found that it mattered all the world to him, and that everything – hope, peace of mind, comfort – was bound up for him with the question of the nature and the rights of Jesus. It is the most momentous of all questions – 'Whom say ye that I am?'

The Gospels make it quite clear why Jesus chose this particular juncture for his question. His reason was that he had something confidential to tell his disciples about the future, a disclosure to make which was bound to test and try their faith to the utmost, but which could now no longer be kept back from them. *He was going to tell them that he saw death coming to him,* coming speedily and coming with fearful shame (Matthew 16:21; Mark 8:31; Luke 9:22). And he may well have wondered – would that disclosure end their loyalty? Would they turn their backs on him as so many others had done, and all his work be wasted? Everything depended on how high their faith in him had risen. If that faith were weak, if it were still a halting, dim, uncertain thing, the shock of the news he had for them would certainly finish it. Clearly for Jesus, no less than for his disciples, it was an hour of crisis.

He began with the impersonal question – 'Whom do men say that I am?' That, at any rate, was not difficult to answer. For on every side, men were saying things about Jesus. A dozen verdicts were abroad. All kinds of rumours and opinions were in the air. Jesus was on every tongue. And people were not only saying things about Jesus; they were saying *great* things about him. Some thought he was John the Baptist back from the dead. Others said he reminded them of Elijah. Others spoke of Jeremiah or another of the prophets. In other words, while current opinions were by no means unanimous as to Jesus' identity, they were unanimous that he was someone great. His place was among the heroes of his race.

It is worth remarking that history is here repeating itself. Once again Jesus is on every tongue. He is being discussed today far beyond the circle of the Christian Church: and great is the diversity of verdicts about him. Papini, looking at Jesus, sees the Poet. Bruce Barton sees the Man of Action. Middleton Murry sees the Mystic. Men with no brief for orthodoxy are ready to extol Jesus as the paragon of saints and captain of all moral leaders for ever. 'Even now,' said John Stuart Mill, 'it would not be easy even for an unbeliever to find a better translation of the rule of virtue from the abstract into the concrete than to endeavour so to live that Christ would approve our life.' Like the people of his own day who called him John, Elijah, Jeremiah, so the people of today are agreed that among the heroes and saints of all time, Jesus stands supreme.

But Jesus was not content with that recognition. People were saying that he was John, Elijah, Jeremiah. But that meant that he was one in a series. It meant that there were precedents and parallels, and that even if he stood first in rank, he was still only *primus inter pares* – first among his equals. But quite certainly that is not what the Christ of the New Testament claimed. People may agree with Christ's claim, or they may dissent from it; but as to the fact of the claim itself there is not a shadow of a doubt. Christ claimed to be something and someone unprecedented, unparalleled, unrivalled, unique (*eg* Matthew 11:27; 10:37; 24:35; John 10:30; 14:6). No doubt the Roman Emperor who had a statue of Jesus and a statue of Plato side by side in his pantheon, thought that he was paying the Master a noble tribute; and indeed, in a sense, he was – only that was not the Gospel. No doubt Ernest Renan, when he wrote of Jesus that 'he stood in the first rank of the grand family of the true sons of God', felt that he was according the Man of Nazareth royal honour and dignity – but again, it was not the Gospel. John the Baptist, Elijah, Jeremiah, Jesus – was that the final truth about the world's redeemer? One in a list? Plato, Socrates, Buddha, Jesus – is that the truth? St Francis, St Bernard, St Augustine, Jesus – is that the truth? People have been content with the answer sometimes: it has never contented Jesus. And so here at Caesarea the 'Whom say men that I am?' was left behind; and straight, swift, direct came this – 'Whom say *ye* that I am?'

Observe how he pushed beyond the impersonal discussion to the personal challenge. That was regularly Christ's way. You can see it in his conversation with the woman at the well – first the general talk, then suddenly the rapier-thrust at her own heart. You can see it in his interview with Pontius Pilate, when the latter was questioning him about his kingly claims. Suddenly, like an arrow, came the challenge: 'Sayest thou this thing of thyself, or did others tell it thee of me?' Is this your own verdict, Pilate, or just rumour that you are retailing at second-hand? Always, sooner or later, Jesus brought things back to the personal issue. He was not anxious for any second-hand opinions or verdicts by proxy. What he wanted was the straight answer of a person's own experience. Whom say *ye* that I am?

It ought here to be said that this question of Jesus is being forced upon the world today from three sides. *History* forces it upon us. This Jesus who 'doth bestride the narrow world like a Colossus' – in a far truer sense than Julius Caesar ever did, or

Alexander, or Napoleon – whose cause had died a score of deaths down the centuries, only to come alive again each time, more glorious than ever – who can he be? *The Bible* forces it upon us. This carpenter's apprentice who could make claims like 'all things are delivered unto me of my Father' (Matthew 11:27); this wandering preacher who could bid the whole labouring, heavy-laden world come to him for rest (verse 28) – who can he be? *Conscience* forces it upon us. This man whose words still stab us like the sword of God, whose eyes still haunt us, whose pure, holy image puts us on our honour to live clean – who can he be? The world has no chance of escaping the question. And everything in religion and in life depends upon the answer.

4 *The* ANSWER *of* FAITH

Simon Peter rose to it. He rose to it with all the daring of his impetuous, loving heart. Try to feel the tense drama of the moment. Here was this question which had never been asked before. Here was the question to which, through long, patient months of personal training and fellowship, Jesus had been leading his men up. He knew that upon the way in which they might answer it, everything for the future of his work depended. And now it was asked. We may well believe that there was silence for a moment, for these twelve men were facing now the ultimate mystery of things and the unfathomable depths of the being of God. But suddenly Peter rose to it, rose above all the poor, levelling, half-believing answers of men, and rang out his own startling, tremendous answer – 'Thou art the Christ, the Son of the living God!'

The question has sometimes been raised as to how much this confession of Peter's implied. Quite certainly it implied a recognition of Jesus as the long-looked-for Messiah of Israel.

Others were ready to hail Jesus as one of the Messiah's heralds. That is what was meant by calling him Elijah and Jeremiah; for the belief was that these great figures of the past were to re-appear upon the earth before the Messianic age broke in. But Peter had caught the truth in a flash. This was no herald. This was the Christ of God himself.

But does the confession of Jesus as Messiah have any relevance today? Was Messiahship not simply an old Jewish idea which has long ceased to be valid? To these questions we must reply that if the word and conception were Jewish, local and temporal, as they undoubtedly were, the thing itself was universal and eternal. For what did the Messianic idea mean but just this: that someone was coming who would be the hope of the world, the fulfilment of every promise, and the answer to every prayer, one who would straighten out all human tangles, and right all earthly wrongs and bring in a better day of God? That was the idea. And we can see that, so far from having lost its meaning by the passing of the years, it has now more meaning than ever. For we are being driven by the very stress of our difficulties to realise that the one hope of the world is the recognition and the acceptance of Jesus as God's guiding word to our generation. Everything depends upon whether we are ready to say with Peter, 'Thou art the Christ'.

5 *The* DIVINITY *of* CHRIST

But did Peter mean more than this? 'Son of the living God,' he said. Now, that would not necessarily mean anything more than Messiah, for we know that in Jewish thought and speech 'Son of God' and 'Messiah' were sometimes synonymous terms. But surely on Peter's lips it did mean something more. Through all these months, something had been happening in the lives of Peter and his fellow-disciples, which none of them until now had dared to put into words: they were beginning to feel towards Jesus just as they had always felt towards God. They found now that when they tried to think of God, it was Jesus' face they saw; and they were glad to make to this Master of theirs that surrender of life which only the God of heaven can legitimately claim from any one. All that went into Peter's cry, 'Thou art the Christ, the Son of the living God'.

There, then, was the great conviction. And we can see now the line along which Peter had reached it. It was the line along which this conviction must still come, if it is to come at all. He came to it *by living in the company of Jesus*. The conviction had not been there to begin with. When Jesus went to Simon the fisherman and said, 'follow me', and when the man rose and followed, he did not fully realise who it was he was following. His only thought then had been, 'Here is the kind of Leader I have been looking for, and I am going with him now'. A very rudimentary faith! Yes, but enough for a beginning. Indeed, it is not possible to expect any more – for a beginning. Jesus never asked any more. He never began by dictating to men what they were to think of him. He never put them through a catechism about his divine claims. The great thing was that people could begin with Jesus anywhere, just where they were. Jesus accepted Peter gladly on these terms, not demanding full belief at once, but waiting for belief to grow and mature.

And grow and mature it did. It was the long days and nights in Jesus' company, mounting into months and years, which ultimately made the man a believer. For every day he was hearing Jesus speak with a strange, incredible authority he had never heard in any voice before. Every day he was watching Jesus at work, and observing with growing admiration and wonder how more than equal he was to all emergencies. Every day he was seeing Jesus in contact with shattered, futile lives, and these lives going back to the world again changed in a way which he had always thought was absolutely impossible for anyone but God to change them. There was more even than that. In his own heart Peter knew that none but God could forgive sin: yet in his own heart there was a voice telling him with utter certainty that this Jesus had forgiven him, and had indeed done more than that, for he was now breaking the power of sin in his servant's life – a work which only the God of heaven could do. That is how Peter found who Christ was. When all is said, how else can anyone find it? This Jesus does for me what only God can do. This Jesus redeems my life as only the Eternal could redeem it. This Jesus floods my being as only the Father of heaven could flood it. What can I do but confess it? This is divine! 'Thou art the Christ, the Son of the living God.'

In the last resort however, Peter's knowledge of the Messiahship and divinity of Christ came as an inward revelation from God. 'Flesh and blood hath not revealed it unto thee, but my Father which is in heaven.' It was not a discovery which the disciple by himself had achieved; and while Peter's quest for the truth had certainly opened up the way for the coming of the vision, yet the vision when it came was God's gift. It was God who had flashed it in upon him. The conviction was not man-made, but God-given. It had come upon Peter with inherent, compelling power, authenticating itself to his heart, so that, apart from any argument, independently of any logical proof or demonstration, the man could say with absolute assurance, 'I know'. Somewhere in Peter's heart God's bell had tolled, and in that moment he knew that in Jesus Christ he was touching the Eternal. Such moments of revelation are the very life of religion. Only God can make us finally sure of God.

6 *The* ROCK

Very significant is the great burst of glowing emotion with which Jesus received his disciple's confession. 'Blessed art thou,

Simon Bar-jona!' Here, felt Jesus, was ample reward for all the patience of the years. Here was something at last to show for the travail of his soul. Here was the assurance that, whatever might happen now – defeat, death, apparent disaster – the cause was safe. And with that, Jesus' heart was lifted up in a great exulting gratitude to God. It is a striking illustration of what one man's faith can mean to our Lord. 'Blessed art thou, Simon. Thou art Peter – a Rock; and upon this rock I will build my church.' It has been debated what Jesus was referring to by the 'rock'. Was it Peter the man? Or was it Peter's confession of faith? Surely it was both. It was on Peter as a believing man, on Peter as a fully surrendered man, that the Church was to be built. But clearly the promise goes far out beyond Peter and the first generation of Christians. It is on believing men and women, on surrendered men and women, down through the years, that Christ has done his building, and it is on them he is building now. Are we the kind of material that Christ can build with? What is our faith and loyalty – drifting, shifting sand, or firm, resolute rock? These are questions which every Christian must face alone with his or her own soul, and with God.

XIV
The Royal Law of Love

1   *A* ROYAL LAW

IT is a royal law *because it is the law of a King*. 'Ye have heard that it hath been said, Thou shalt ... hate thine enemy. But I say unto you, [listen to the kingly authority of Jesus!] Love your enemies' (Matthew 5:43f).

It is a royal law *because it takes precedence of every other law*. If we fail here, says Jesus, we fail all along the line. No imposing array of splendid virtues, no deep piety nor long prayers, have any weight at all with God if the spirit of love is lacking (Matthew 5:23f). This is God's ultimate test of the reality of our religion. 'If a man has not the love of God shed abroad in his heart,' cried D L Moody, 'he has never been regenerated.' 'He that loveth not knoweth not God; for God is love' (I John 4:8).

It is a royal law *because to obey it makes life royally happy*. 'With what measure ye mete,' said Jesus, 'it shall be measured to you again' (Matthew 7:2). That means an uncharitable attitude is a boomerang: it comes back on a person who uses it. But it means also that as surely as an unloving spirit towards others poisons in the long run the atmosphere of a person's own life, so surely does a loving spirit sweeten it. Every one comes ultimately to inhabit the kind of world he makes for himself; and it is only the person who lives by love who can taste the gladness of God.

2 LOVE'S MEANING

What kind of love was it that Jesus commanded and extolled? Certainly not a genial amiability and good nature with no moral backbone, no power of standing up to the biting east winds of truth. Certainly not an all-inclusive toleration which allows the eternal distinctions of right and wrong to be blurred. The Christ who could speak the terrible words about the mill-stone and the depths of the sea (Matthew 18:6), the Christ of the whip of cords (Matthew 21:12; John 2:15), never counselled an easy-going benevolence indifferent to moral values. That is not Christian love: that is un-Christian laziness. What Jesus did mean by love was a spirit that never harbours a grudge, because it is much too big for that kind of pettiness; that always discovers the best in mankind, because it can see underground; that is full of understanding, because it has been through hard places itself; wonderfully patient, because it has a great hope at its heart; utterly pure, because it knows God.

'Judge not, that ye be not judged' (Matthew 7:1) does not mean (as easy-going good nature might suggest) throwing our critical faculty overboard (cf John 7:24: 'Judge righteous judgement'). Jesus would have said 'Amen' to the Psalmist's injunction – 'Ye that love the Lord, hate evil' (Psalm 97:10). Leave out the moral stringency of Jesus, and you are not left with the Jesus of the New Testament. In any case, we are to be stern in judging ourselves; as St Augustine said greatly, 'To my God, a heart of flame; to my fellow men, a heart of love; to myself, a heart of steel'.

3 LOVE'S NECESSITY

Wherever Jesus went, he found hearts that were hungry for love. On the jaded face of Zacchaeus (Luke 19:5), in the glib talk of a Samaritan woman (John 4:10ff), in the weary looks of an inarticulate, shepherdless crowd (Matthew 9:36), that hunger for love struck at Christ's own heart. Hence he laid it down that while men did not need many qualifications to be his disciples, no man could be a disciple who was not prepared to love. The heart of the world was crying for love.

According to Jesus, the real foe of God – in Church, in State, in individual – has always been lovelessness. Self is Antichrist. The selfish attitude is one of those respectable sins which (just because they are respectable, in contrast with certain sins of the flesh) society in Jesus' day and society today have been apt to overlook. Yet to this sin more than any other, whether of the flesh or the mind, the eyes of Jesus are 'as a flame of fire' (Revelation 1:14). Many things Jesus can forgive: lovelessness he cannot tolerate.

4 LOVE'S METHOD

There is an unkind way of being 'kind', an unloving way of being 'loving'. This was Jesus' charge against the Pharisees. They sounded a trumpet when they did their alms (Matthew 6:1, 2). Their love was forced. It was professional, official, unnatural. It used words that did not come from the heart. Suffused with a warm glow of conscious virtue, it was none the less counterfeit. It rang false. And the people to whom a love like that was shown, could nearly always detect the flaw in it. That was why it hurt them. That was why it was worse than sheer indifference. Real love, said Jesus, makes no parade (Matthew 6:3, 4; cf I Corinthians 13:4). It is not a forced nor a patronising thing, but the natural outflow of a God-filled heart.

Jesus' own attitude is decisive here. His deeds of love were done quietly (Mark 8:23, 26 – note specially 'led him out of the town'; Luke 5:14). His love was never condescending. He loved mankind, not because it was a duty, but because he could not help it (Mark 10:21). He made himself mankind's brother, not because he was in the world to promote brotherhood, but because he found people so lovable. Official love is a poor and shabby thing compared with the love of Jesus.

5 LOVE'S DIFFICULTY

With Jesus' law of love itself, the disciples most heartily agreed; the trouble began when they tried to apply it in the practical relationships of life. There the trouble always begins. Let us get this clear. We agree with Jesus that love is the greatest thing in the world (Matthew 22:40); but if in home or business we are irritable, then our religion is thoroughly unreal. We may assent to every word Jesus says in the Gospels about forgiveness; but if we cannot forget that So-and-so slighted us, or neglected to consult us sufficiently, or said something hard about us, we are nowhere near Jesus at all. Even in the first disciple band, love sometimes broke down. Questions of precedence divided them (Matthew 18:1; Mark 9:34; Luke 22:24). Rivalries sprang up (Matthew 20:21, 24). One day none of them would stoop to wash the others' feet (John 13:4, 5). Feelings of independence and personal rights asserted themselves, and love was ousted.

Jesus' attitude to this matter of independence is perfectly clear. It is the antithesis of the world's attitude. The world says that to declare, when someone has hurt you, that you are going to stand up for your rights and 'get even', is to show your independence. Jesus says it shows a radical *lack* of independence. It shows you are not independent enough to rise above the hurting thing. You are its slave, not its master. This is the teaching of the Sermon on the Mount (Matthew 5:38-48). It is the teaching of Christ's whole life, 'who when he was reviled, reviled not again' (I Peter 2:23; cf Mark 14:65). When love and personal independence appear to collide, it must be a false independence; and there cannot be a moment's doubt as to which of the two things – our apparent independence, or Christ's demand of love – must give way. But that is where the struggle comes in. That is one of the difficulties of love.

Another difficulty, real to the first disciples and real today, is this. Can mankind really live by the law of love, as Jesus pledged his followers to live, in a world where that law is not acknowledged? Can they take that risk? Clearly if we were all to agree to accept Christ's command, and were to begin simultaneously putting that command into practice, the practice of it would be easy. But dare Christians begin now, in a world that has no intention of beginning? It would not be nearly so hard for one person here to act lovingly towards another there, if he could be quite sure in advance that the other would act in the same way towards him: but for the first to act lovingly towards the second, *and risk the rest* – there's the rub. But certainly it was nothing less than that which Jesus asked. His own love never waited to be sure. It plunged right in. It took the risk. It was while we were still enemies, says St Paul, that he died for us (Romans 5:10). It was on the Cross, where the world killed him, that he pled for the world's forgiveness (Luke 23:34).

This is a main part of the adventure of Christianity. Living by love in a world like this is bound to be a risk. And Jesus never tried to conceal the risk of it (Luke 21:12). He made the very risk of it his challenge, especially to youth. Everything that was honourable and gallant in youth, he felt sure, would rise to the challenge. And he was not disappointed. It did rise to it. It is rising to it today. Love's difficulty is love's glory.

6 LOVE'S LENGTH

The test of love is the length to which it is prepared to go.

Christ's own love went the length of Calvary. And when he bade Peter forgive his brother, not seven times, but seventy times seven (Matthew 18:21f), he meant that true love would acknowledge no limits whatever. Did Christ ask too much? Did he pitch his demands too high? The criticism has been urged that Jesus' teaching on love is idealistic, impracticable for this rough competitive world, not humanly possible. To that criticism the Gospels return two answers. On the one hand, a Christian exists to attempt the impossible (Matthew 19:26; Mark 9:23). On the other hand, the complaint that Jesus expects too much of human nature, and that there are lengths to which it is not 'humanly possible' for love to go, is beside the point. Jesus never said that his religion would be human in that sense. He never suggested that his demands would be humanly possible (Matthew 5:20, 48). He said that the glory of his religion was that there was something in it not human at all, but *super*human, and that it would set men transcending the humanly possible by an inward urge that was divine. 'The truth is,' as H G Wells has said, 'the Galilean has been too great for our small hearts.'

Hence the law of love is closely linked with the law of cross-bearing (Matthew 16:24). Quite frankly, Jesus said that any one who accepts the former will sometimes have to face self-crucifixion. And no one has a right to sing, 'Jesus, I my cross have taken', and yet complain that the law of love and forgiveness unto seventy times seven is asking too much of him or her. This *is* the Cross. Love meant Calvary to Jesus. And 'the disciple is not above his Master' (Matthew 10:24).

7 LOVE'S MOTIVE

Jesus never asked his men to do anything for which he did not also supply the power. What he called for, he helped to create. When he laid down the royal law of love, he supplied along with it the necessary dynamic. In the Gospels three master-motives emerge.

Jesus created love *by revealing the essential dignity and lovableness of mankind.* It is easy to notice a person's shabby coat, his defects in grammar, his peculiar ways: Jesus went deeper, and showed that every soul was a potential son or daughter of a king. Of a scorned, renegade tax-gatherer, he said, 'He also is a son of Abraham' (Luke 19:9). A woman whom all good people ostracised, he treated with a dignity and courtesy that might have been given to a queen (Luke 7:37ff). And when he said, 'Take heed that ye despise not one of these little ones' (Matthew 18:10), he was thinking, not only of the children, but of all the weak, defenceless, sensitive things of life. It does most mightily inspire love towards your fellow men and women when you can see, as Jesus saw, upon every face that passes you in the street, something of the image of God.

Jesus created love *by dying for mankind.* Every day of his life the disciples saw their Master squandering his strength for the sick and the sinful, and when Calvary came they knew that it was for sheer love of them that he had died. Can you continue to be unloving to any one, even the most unlovable, when you remind yourself, 'It was for that person Jesus died'?

Here lies the real motive for international peace. The person who says he does not believe in peace, who thinks that patriotism means his country before all others, his rights at all costs to be upheld, even though it means trampling someone else's rights underfoot – that person is not only guilty of foolishness: he is guilty of making the Cross of Christ of none effect. For it was on that Cross that Christ died for love of mankind. Hence, in our generation, the work of peace must be something more than the mere hobby of a group of Christians: it is every Christian's plain duty to Christ. And the Cross is the motive and the driving-power.

Jesus created love *by flooding human hearts with his own spirit.*

Forgiveness to seventy times seven might be quite out of the question for a man of Peter's temperament to achieve. But what Peter discovered was that it was not out of the question for *Christ in him* to achieve. He began by trying to make himself love his fellow-disciples, and he found that this was hopeless. But as the days went on, he allowed Christ more and more to flood his heart, and then love for the brethren came of its own accord. As Temple Gairdner of Cairo put it, changing by a single letter the great dictum of St Paul, 'Not I, but Christ loveth in me'.

This is still today the crux of the matter. 'Other men,' said a brilliant German about Goethe, 'I love with my own strength, but he teaches me to love with his strength.' Is there anyone you think you could never love? But Christ could love him or her. Why should not Christ in you do it? He teaches you to love with his strength. That is the secret.

8 LOVE'S POWER

It was Jesus who first proved that love, which in a world given over to force looks the weakest of weapons, is in reality the strongest. Love gains victories which the hard, critical, censorious attitude never gains. The Pharisaic attitude to shamed and broken sinners never had and never has any redeeming power about it. Indeed, it works all the other way, and serves only to bind on the fetters of bitterness and despair more securely than ever. 'God, I thank thee,' said the Pharisee of Jesus' parable, 'that I am not as other men are, extortioners, unjust, adulterers, or even as this publican' (Luke 18:11). That is loveless religion, entirely powerless to bring any soul into the Kingdom. But Jesus loved the publican, and by loving him gave him back his manhood and his self-respect, brought the cowed, shamed soul on to his feet again, put the light of hope into his eyes, and saved him. If Peter after his denial had been met with hard censoriousness, in all probability there would never have been a St Peter in Scripture today. But the love of Jesus, which even after that most terrible failure went on loving him (Mark 16:7; John 21:15), lifted him right out of the fearful pit of his sin and the miry clay of despair, and set his feet on the rock again. And here Jesus was a pattern for all his followers for ever. Love is not only better than criticism: it is also infinitely more effectual. It is redeeming power.

An old fable tells that in all the world there was only one thing that could melt adamant, one liquid potent enough to dissolve the everlasting rock, and that was blood from a human heart. Is there not something more than a fable there? 'If I go through the fire,' says the St Joan of Bernard Shaw's play, 'I shall go through it to their hearts for ever and ever.' So love takes its very defeats and out of them forges the weapon of victory. It is the weakness of God which is stronger than all the force of men (I Corinthians 1:25).

9 LOVE'S REWARD

Love, just because it is love, asks no reward. All that it asks is to be allowed to go on loving more and more. The whole idea of taking the Christian way for the sake of regard is alien to Jesus' mind. 'When ye shall have done all those things which are commanded you, say, we are unprofitable servants' (Luke 17:10). Yet a reward there is. Certainly lovelessness reaps its recompense. The hard, censorious spirit reacts upon the person who shows it, and he finds himself at last inhabiting a loveless desert of a world. Moreover, the unforgiving spirit, said Jesus, goes unforgiven, because it is ultimately unforgivable. The great parable of the servant whose debt to the king was remitted, but who would not remit a fellow-servant's debt to himself (Matthew 18:23-34), ends with the solemn words, 'So likewise shall my heavenly Father do also unto you, if ye from your hearts forgive not every one his brother their trespasses' (Matthew 18:35). The loveless spirit is not excluded, it excludes itself, from reconciliation and fellowship with God.

But if lovelessness 'has its reward', there is also a rich reward for love. Jesus' familiar principle, 'Unto every one which hath shall be given' (Luke 19:26), holds good here; for love is a creative thing, and reproduces itself in others, and returns to the person who lives by it. Even a cup of cold water, if given for the love of Jesus, brings blessing to the person who gave it (Matthew 10:42); every gift to the least of the Lord's brethren is a gift to the Lord himself (Matthew 25:40). Moreover, to exercise forgiving love, said Jesus, is to put yourself in the way of God's forgiveness: it is to live in the only sphere in which the cleansing pardon of heaven can operate (Matthew 6:12, 14). But the great reward of the loving spirit is none of God's gifts, but God himself (John 14:23). The person who loves is creating the atmosphere in which the Spirit of God can dwell: and the Spirit comes, and tabernacles in that human life, and makes that soul his home. So love is crowned. The Lord is there.

We are of Thee, the children of Thy love,
The brothers of Thy well-beloved Son;
Descend, O Holy Spirit, like a dove,
Into our hearts, that we may be as one;
As one with Thee, to whom we ever tend;
As one with Him, our Brother and our Friend.

XV
Jesus and Social Questions

1 *The* ATTITUDE *of the* MASTER

WE have now to inquire what we can learn from the Gospels about the attitude of Jesus to the social questions of his day and of our own. Two widely divergent views have appeared. On the one hand, it is suggested that Jesus did not concern himself with social questions at all. On the other hand, he has been hailed as the world's greatest social reformer. It is necessary to examine these positions.

According to the former, Jesus' exclusive preoccupation was the soul. He taught a mystical piety. He was content to leave material conditions just as he found them. He deliberately refused to take cognisance of any aspects of the life of mankind in the world except the spiritual. He came, not to save the world as it was, but to save men out of the world. He was not concerned with the redress of social wrongs or the reform of social injustice: his thoughts were moving on another plane. This view has led some of Jesus' followers in every age of the Church to make a complete divorce between their religion and their social duties, with the regrettable result that Christianity has sometimes appeared to those outside to be indifferent or even hostile to reform, and has been accused of buttressing old abuses.

It is a totally mistaken view. Even a cursory examination of the Gospels shows how wide of the mark it is. Jesus came preaching a *kingdom,* and the very use of that idea raised profound social issues. He proclaimed a Gospel of brotherhood. He gathered his first followers into a social unit, with a real communal life. The Sermon on the Mount is full of social teaching. His healing miracles, as we have already discussed (see chapter XI, 'The Ministry of Healing'), sprang from his passionate desire to help people physically *and* spiritually. The hardships of the poor were never a matter of indifference to Jesus (Matthew 9:36). True, he declared that 'man shall not live by bread alone' (Matthew 4:4). But neither shall man live without any bread at all, and Jesus always remembered that; and in the heart of the great prayer he taught his disciples, he found a place for it: 'Give us this day our daily bread' (Matthew 6:11).

Mankind's material wants, far from being matters of no moment, were actually written upon the heart of God: 'Your heavenly Father knoweth that ye have need of all these things' (Matthew 6:32). Indeed, the whole tendency to distinguish between sacred and secular concerns in life is thoroughly alien to the Gospels. Jesus claimed the whole of life for his province. His religion was to invade every corner of a person's experience, every department of public and private life, every nook and cranny of the world. Everything was to come under the sweep of the one Spirit. No one was to be able to draw a line and say, 'Here Christ's authority stops. Thus far, Jesus, no further. The rest is beyond your sway!' Dual control of that kind, Jesus insisted, would always imply a radical insincerity. For there cannot ultimately be two kinds of truth: there is only one. Either Jesus must be king everywhere, or he has no place at all. The only alternatives are to apply his religion to every single one of life's relationships, or else drop that religion altogether: there is no third option. This is the whole trend of Jesus' teaching in the Gospels. This is the claim of Christianity.

The view which regards social questions as outside Jesus'

scope must accordingly be abandoned. But equally wide of the mark is the opposite view, which hails Jesus as primarily a social reformer. This view holds that the first step towards a redeemed humanity must be a redeemed social order. Improve external conditions, it says, then the Spirit of God will have a chance. Eliminate poverty and ignorance, then it will be comparatively easy to eliminate sin. But quite certainly this was not Christ's line of approach. For one thing, Jesus was quite clear that the Kingdom could never be built by human effort: it was to be the act of God. Moreover, Jesus saw, and openly declared, that changed conditions were futile without changed hearts (Matt. 15:19f). Hence his refusal of the short-cuts suggested by the Tempter in the wilderness (Matthew 4:1ff). People would never be right with one another until they were first right with God. The real trouble of humanity was too deep-seated to be reached by any social remedies or improved conditions; and if Jesus was a great reformer, it was because he was a Saviour first.

Somewhere between the two views we have examined, the real truth of the matter lies. Jesus came with a social message for his age and for every age. But the basis of that message was not social, but religious. His influence upon world conditions has been a consequence of his revelation of God. He headed no social revolution, he legislated for no current social problems: but he brought and imparted a spirit that was bound to set people crusading against social injustice everywhere.

It is in this way that Jesus has been the driving power of all noble social service over the centuries. The Spirit of Jesus touched the institution of slavery, laid an axe to the root of that accursed tree whose branches had been darkening the heavens, robbing millions of God's good sunshine, and down the tree came crashing. The Spirit of Jesus, working through Lord Shaftesbury and others, touched the appalling factory conditions of the nineteenth century, and showed them up, and put something better and more decent in their place. The Spirit of Jesus touched the tragedy of unrelieved distress and pain, and everywhere hospitals and homes of healing sprang into existence; every infirmary in the land today has been built by Jesus Christ. Always it has been through changed men and women that Jesus has changed the world. Always the highest social impetus has had that religious basis. And the Church is not only truest to its own origins and closest to its own Gospel, it is also strongest as a power for social good, when, while speaking out boldly for social righteousness, it concentrates on its own God-appointed task, *and holds up Christ.*

Keeping this in mind, we shall now look briefly at one or two of the great social relationships on which the life and teaching of Jesus have cast a light.

2 FAMILY LIFE

Jesus himself belonged to a people among whom the institution of the family was more highly honoured than in any other nation of the world. Various causes had contributed to this high estimate of the family among the Jews. One was the conviction that family life was a divine creation: the prologue of Genesis preserved the story of its origin, and showed that it sprang straight out of the mind of God (Genesis 1:26; 2:18). Hence it became natural to regard each separate family as a religious organism; and, in a very deep sense, every Jewish father was a priest in his own home (Deuteronomy 16:11). Moreover, the Jewish law had played an important part in maintaining the purity of family life. Admittedly the law, in many of its aspects, was a yoke of bondage; but it stands to its credit that it did preserve Judaism from the moral landslide which was happening throughout the rest of the world. Nor must it be forgotten that many a Hebrew mother cherished the secret hope that her son might be the Messiah. This was a favourite interpretation of certain Old Testament prophecies, and it is obvious that such a hope must have helped mightily to keep family life sound and pure.

But Jesus invested family life with an even deeper sanctity. He did this in three ways.

He himself lived for the greater part of his life in the heart of a family (see chapter III, 'Childhood and Youth'). He had four brothers and at least two sisters (Matthew 13:55ff). For thirty years the glory of God was content to tabernacle in a peasant home. Hence family life has been hallowed for ever.

Further, *Jesus regarded the family as a miniature of the Kingdom of God.* This comes out in his constant use of family relationships to illustrate and drive home some of his profoundest spiritual truths. It was from the life of the family that Jesus drew his supreme conception of the divine nature: God, he said, is a Father. The greatest of all the parables is a story of home life (Luke 15:11ff). Forgiveness, as experienced within the intimate relationships of home, is a wonderful interpreter of the forgiveness of God. The human family becomes a microcosm of the heavenly Kingdom.

Finally, *Jesus deepened the sanctity of the family by what he did for womanhood and childhood.* Here it is not so much definite teaching of Jesus that we have to go upon, as his whole attitude. By his attitude to the women of the Gospel story, Jesus has emancipated womanhood and crowned it with dignity and honour. Even the lofty Jewish standards were far transcended here. Of marriage, Jesus said, 'What therefore God hath joined together, let not man put asunder' (Mark 10:9). Paul was thoroughly true to the spirit of his Master when he declared that in Christ 'there is neither male nor female' (Galatians 3:28).

Childhood, too, came under Jesus' transfiguring touch. One particular day he 'called a little child unto him, and set him in the midst' (Matthew 18:2); and the child-life has been in the midst ever since. How vast the revolution there has been, may be strikingly illustrated from the contents of an old papyrus letter, dating from the beginning of the Christian era, which came to light during excavations. It is a letter written by a husband on foreign service to his wife at home, and its exact date is, significantly, the year 1 BC: 'Let me tell you that we are still in Alexandria. I beg you to look after the child, and as soon as we get wages I will send you something. If it is a boy, let it alone. If it is a girl, throw it away.' Into a world tolerant of that utter callousness came Jesus, and, taking childhood to his heart, declared that of such was the Kingdom of God (Mark 10:14).

But while Jesus thus deepened immeasurably the sanctity of family life, he was careful to point out that, in certain circumstances, the claims of home must be relegated to a secondary place. There came a point in his own life when the home of his youth in Nazareth could keep him no longer, and the clinging hands had to be gently set aside. Later, when his mother and brethren sought him out and begged to speak with him, he could only answer, 'Whosoever shall do the will of my Father ... the same is my brother, and sister, and mother' (Matthew 12:50). Nor did he hesitate to ask a similar renunciation from the men he chose as disciples. On one occasion, describing the disruptive effect his challenge would have on human society, he said, 'I am come to set a man at variance against his father, and the daughter against her mother, and the daughter-in-law against her mother-in-law' (Matthew 10:35). When a potential recruit to his cause made the suggestion, 'Lord, I will follow thee; but let me first go bid them farewell which are at home at my house', Jesus, seeing apparently the timid resolution which the treaties of home would all too easily break, refused the proffered service and turned sadly away (Luke 9:61).

Great as Jesus recognised the claims of home to be, he never hesitated to assert that if ever these claims and the claims of God should be at variance, God's claims must come first. The practical bearings of this demand, in the early days of Christianity, when the new religion was making its way and families were divided over it and persecution was hot, were obvious and far-reaching, as they still are in non-Christian lands where the Gospel is proclaimed today. But even in our own Christian land, and in our own lives, this ruling of Jesus carries weight. When lesser loyalties conflict with larger, he says, a person must ensure that the latter prevail. A Christian must be ready, if guided by God, to surrender even the call of home for the Kingdom's sake.

3   WEALTH *and* POVERTY

The frequency of allusion in the Gospels to money may at first sight seem surprising. Take the parables. Here is one about a wealthy landowner whose profits had grown so embarrassingly large that he found the disposal of them a real problem; the parable relates how he solved that problem to his own satisfaction, and what God thought of his solution (Luke 12:16ff). Here is another about a money-lender whose junior assistant, having turned out to be a lazy, good-for-nothing scamp, was about to be dismissed, but who managed by altering certain accounts to ingratiate himself with some of his master's influential customers; and the parable ends with the strange saying about 'making friends with the mammon of unrighteousness' (Luke 16:1ff). Here is another about a wealthy Syrian Jew, an honest, decent man in his own way, but far too busy managing his own affairs and entertaining his own friends to have any thoughts for a beggar lying at his back door (Luke 16:19ff).

In the following parables, money finds a place: the Hidden Treasure (Matthew 13:44ff); the Unmerciful Servant (Matthew 18:23ff); the Labourers in the Vineyard (Matthew 20:1ff); the Two Debtors (Luke 7:41ff); the Good Samaritan (Luke 10:30ff); the Lost Coin (Luke 15:8ff); and the Ten Pounds (Luke 19:11ff).

Quite apart from the parables, too, money enters largely into the Gospel story: notably in such incidents as the interview with the rich young ruler (Matthew 19:16ff); the conversion of Zacchaeus (Luke 19:1ff); and the gift which the poor widow made to God (Mark 12:41ff).

Now this frequency of allusion might seem surprising until we remember how inextricably the whole question of money gets mixed up with the lives and experience of ordinary men and women in this world, even against their will. It gets mixed up even with fine, spiritual things – like the love of parents for their children, or the compassion of a Good Samaritan for the distress of his neighbour, or the thank-offering a man makes to God. Jesus was no fanciful dreamer, dwelling in the clouds: Jesus was a realist, and saw the facts as they were. Here, then, was a whole aspect of life which could not be ignored. Here was a clamant need for all the guidance he could give. Let us see the direction which that guidance took.

It is clear, to begin with, that *Jesus did not say that possessions of any kind were necessarily and intrinsically wrong.* Among his own followers he numbered at least one rich man, Joseph of Arimathaea (Matthew 27:57ff). His circle of friends included some who, if not wealthy, were certainly quite well-to-do – such people as Nicodemus (John 3:1ff); and the centurion of Capernaum (Luke 7:2ff); and the family at Bethany (Luke 10:38ff); and his nameless host in Jerusalem (Mark 14:13ff); and the women who 'ministered unto him of their substance' (Luke 8:3). The moral of the tale of the Rich Man and Lazarus, as Jesus told it, was certainly not that the rich man was sent to torment for being rich, and the poor man rewarded with heaven for being poor: Lazarus was in Abraham's bosom in heaven, and Abraham was one of the richest men who ever lived (Luke 16:19ff). And when Jesus demanded of the rich young ruler that he should sell everything and strip himself bare of all possessions, he was not laying down a universal law, but he was striking at the thing which, in this particular case, happened to be blocking a soul's road to the Kingdom (Matthew 19:21). Jesus did not say that all possessions were intrinsically evil.

Nor did he teach that poverty is necessarily blessed. Certainly Jesus was poor himself. He was a homeless wanderer (Luke 9:58). He had to borrow the coin he used for an illustration (Matthew 22:19). When he died, he left no possessions behind him for people to divide, except the robe which he had worn (Matthew 27:35). They buried him in another man's tomb (Matthew 27:60). But the poverty of Jesus, like that of his great latter-day follower, Francis of Assissi, was a noble, liberating thing, full of the beauty of the songs of birds, and the flowers, and the flying clouds, and the open road, and the grace of God.

Very different is the poverty of an industrial civilisation, with all its attendant miseries of sordidness and squalor. No glorification of this can be found in the Gospels. The Spirit of Jesus is at work in the world to end such misery, and to secure to every one the opportunity of fulness of life. No unbiased student of the Gospels can fail to see that, while Jesus stood apart from economic disputes, his constant insistence on love and brotherhood implied, in the economic sphere, a demand that the gifts of God which people possessed should be distributed in such a way that all God's children might share the privilege of a life full and free and satisfying. This demand is plainly involved in the very nature of the Gospel. It is an inescapable part of Christ's meaning for the world.

On the positive side, Jesus taught that *possessions must always be regarded as a sacred trust.* Every one is accountable to God for the use which he or she makes of them (Luke 19:12ff). Everything we have received is from God (Matthew 5:45). We are all God's stewards. Nothing is more certain to bring God's judgement and condemnation in the end than a selfish attitude to the good things of this world (Matthew 25:41ff).

Jesus always insisted that *if a person's possessions are beginning to injure his soul, drastic sacrifices are necessary.* Better cut off a right hand than quench the Spirit. Better go into the Kingdom of heaven a pauper, than die a rich man with a pile of gold and a shrivelled, beggared soul. 'What shall it profit a man, if he shall gain the whole world, and lose his own soul?' (Mark 9:36).

Jesus held that *it was easier for a person to be a Christian, if he did not have many possessions.* Wealth might not be unlawful, but certainly it was dangerous. Riches might be nobly and worthily used, but it took a special measure of God's grace to do it. It is here that the main emphasis of Jesus' teaching about money falls. Again and again it is the peril of the thing that he dwells upon. It is apt to give a person a false sense of security. It indisposes him to the acceptance of a sacrificial life. It tends to tone down his moral standards and blunt the edge of conscience. It may become a person's master-passion, a thing be bows down to and worships, thus usurping the place of God himself. There is no mistaking the note of solemn warning in the words, 'It is easier for a camel to go through the eye of a needle, than for a rich man to enter into the kingdom of God' (Matthew 19:24). Riches, said Jesus, are a terrible temptation: thank God if you do not have to meet it!

Finally, Jesus always reminded people that *the best things in life cannot be bought or sold.* He said that 'a man's life' – the inmost secret of existence, the radiant, throbbing splendour that God intended for all his children – 'consisteth not in the abundance of the things which he possesseth' (Luke 12:15). You cannot buy love, or a quiet conscience, or the laughter of children, or the care of the heavenly Father. The great things, the things that make life, are not for purchase; they are 'without money and without price', and have nothing to do with wealth at all. But they have everything to do with a person's self-surrender to God and his or her acceptance of the yoke of Jesus.

4 *The* STATE *and* POLITICS

Here the crucial passage for consideration is the story of the Pharisees' challenge to Jesus on the question of the tribute-money, leading to the memorable declaration about Caesar's rights and God's (Matthew 22:15ff). Let us examine the incident.

The question put to Jesus was a deliberate trap. 'Then went the Pharisees,' says the Evangelist, 'and took counsel how they might entangle him in his talk.' Their idea was that if only they could drive Jesus into an obvious inconsistency and con-tradiction, they would greatly discredit his cause. They were not concerned to get at the truth: their one aim was to down their opponent. And no doubt the task seemed easy enough. After all, was not Jesus an unlettered peasant? Would it not be a simple matter to lead him out of his depth?

They baited their trap with flattery. 'Master,' they began, 'we know that thou art true, and teachest the way of God in truth.' They had yet to learn that the keen eyes of Jesus could pierce any mask! They brought out their problem. 'Is it lawful to give tribute unto Caesar, or not? Ought we to pay the civil tax?'

The trap was cleverly devised. It seemed that, whatever answer Jesus might choose to make, they had him caught. They saw that if Jesus answered 'yes', the chances were that loyal Jews, smarting under Roman taxes and reparation burdens, would be finished with him at once. On the other hand, if he answered 'no', he would be open to a charge of sedition, and Rome would no doubt suppress him. Moreover, if he kept silent, the people around would naturally construe it to mean that he did not know, and that therefore he was not a real prophet at all. Or if he hesitated, and asked for time to consider the matter, telling them to return next day for an answer, that too would undermine his influence altogether. The trap had been most subtly prepared.

But Jesus broke right through it and discomfited them. 'Show me the tribute money,' he demanded. And when the coin was presented, 'Whose is this image and superscription?' he asked. 'Caesar's,' was the answer. 'Render therefore unto Caesar the things which are Caesar's, and unto God the things that are God's.' Give Caesar what belongs to him: give God what belongs to God.

That great saying has suffered from many strange inter-pretations. Some have founded on it a theory of the divine right of kings. Others, at the opposite extreme, have argued from it that the State has no rights at all over the truly religious man. Others, missing the whole point, have treated it as an evasion. What is the true interpretation?

One thing is immediately clear. *Jesus was here refusing to give a cheap, one-sided answer in the debate on party politics.* To have been a combatant in that arena would almost certainly have meant giving his message to the world a partisan appearance, thus obscuring the essential revelation he came to bring. More-over, the political situation of his age, as of every age, was transient and ephemeral, and his purpose was to set it in the light of certain eternally valid laws. In any case, guiding prin-ciples, not detailed instructions, were Christ's concern, and his presence amongst men had a loftier aim than the ending of political debate or the finalising of economic programmes. He came to impart to people a spirit by the power of which they would settle their own debates and work out their own pro-grammes. For the Christian, this of course implies involvement on the political and economic levels.

But while Jesus refused to be drawn into political debate, his words 'Render unto Caesar the things which are Caesar's' imply that *privilege always carries obligation with it*. If you are indebted to the State, then it is a moral duty to honour that debt, just as you would honour any other. The very fact that these men were using Caesar's money implied that they were availing themselves of the services of Caesar's rule: hence, said Jesus, they were bound to accept their responsibility and pay Caesar what they owed him. Privileges of citizenship have corresponding obligations, and Jesus has no approval for the individual who declines his civic duties. In short, the issues at stake, under Jesus' touch, cease to be purely political, and are seen to be moral and religious. Duty, wherever it occurs, is a sacred thing, and must be treated as such. 'Render unto Caesar the things which are Caesar's.'

'And unto God the things that are God's.' Were Jesus' thoughts going back to the great Hebrew conception of the creation of man – 'made in the image of God'? (Genesis 1:27). Tertullian thought so. Caesar's image was on the coin, God's image was on the soul. However worn and blurred and defaced the human coin might become out in the world's currency, the image of the God to whom it belonged was still there. Thus, through all the tangle and undergrowth of the vexed social and political questions of his day, and of every day, Jesus cuts down to eternal fact. He brings everything back to the question of personal surrender. You belong to God, he says. Your bodies, your souls, your minds, your affections – they are all stamped with the divine image. Honour your debt, then! Give God what is his due.

XVI
The Gathering Storm

1 *The* SHADOW *of the* CROSS

ONE of Holman Hunt's most famous paintings, 'The Shadow of
Death', depicts Jesus in the carpenter's workshop at Nazareth.
It is the close of day, and the last rays of the setting sun are
streaming in through the open door. The young carpenter, who
has been toiling at the bench, raises himself for a moment from
his cramped, stooping position, and stretches out his arms. Just
then the dying sun catches his figure and casts his shadow on the
wall behind him; and its form is the form of a cross. It is the
artist's striking way of reminding us that, right from the beginning of Jesus' ministry, death was in the air. From the very
start, the end was certain.

That indeed is evident to anyone who reads between the
lines of the Gospels. In the hour when Jesus, out in the wilderness of the Temptation, flatly and finally rejected the line of
compromise; when he settled it once and for all that his attitude to the world powers and spiritual wickedness in high places
was to be one of uncompromising downright defiance (chapter
V, 'The Desert') – in that hour the shadow of the Cross fell.

Even before then, in the quiet seclusion of the silent years,
Jesus may have seen that sinister shadow from afar. For, as he
studied the Scriptures and came to see himself mirrored in the
figure of the Suffering Servant in Isaiah 53, the thought must
have possessed him that to render a perfect obedience to God, to

make a full life-surrender, was certain, in a world which denied God and stoned the prophets, to lead to suffering and ultimately death. The shadow of the Cross was there from the first.

By the time of the great confession at Caesarea Philippi, it was something more than a shadow. Jesus now began to speak quite explicitly about his coming death. Direct and clear as his words were, however, they failed to stab the disciples fully awake to the truth. The thing, to these men, was incredible! It was against all their preconceived ideas and hopes. It must be some strange parable their Master was telling them – not the literal truth. 'Lord,' exclaimed Peter, 'this shall not be unto thee'; whereupon Jesus, realising that even his best friends would fain interfere with his doing of God's will, replied, 'Get thee behind me, Satan!' (Matthew 16:23). How difficult it was for Jesus to get them to grasp the dreaded truth, may be seen from the fact that, after all this, they could still go on babbling about the best places in the kingdom (Matthew 18:1; 20:20ff), and even more from the fact that, when the blow did fall, it found them amazed and staggered and utterly despairing (Matthew 26:31, 56). Only Christ saw the Cross steadily, and went unwavering to meet it.

2 *The* OPPOSITION *of the* PHARISEES

We have now to watch the gathering storm, and to probe the motives of the hostility which culminated at Calvary. Let us look first at the Pharisees, for it was from their side that the main attack upon the life and character of Jesus was launched.

History has produced some strange anomalies. Never did it produce a stranger one than when it decreed that the men who were, outwardly at least, the most religious people in the land, should be the head and front of the opposition that compassed the death of the Son of God. The Pharisees, who were the true successors of reformers under Ezra and Nehemiah, had set themselves the task of keeping religion alive and strong and uncontaminated in dark and difficult days, and well they had acquitted themselves as defenders of the faith. Righteousness was their keynote, the honour of the one true God their constant theme, and their law (as we saw in our discussion of family life) had kept the moral standard high. Yet to Pharisaism, Jesus was anathema. Why?

Three sources of their hatred stand out clearly in the story. The first was that *they believed Jesus to be an impostor*. Hopes of a Messiah ran high among the Pharisees, and when Jesus sprang to sudden popularity they could not ignore him. Even though he did not openly declare himself, his movement seemed to be assuming Messianic proportions. But the possibility that the Deliverer of Israel might arise, as Jesus had, from the ranks of the poor, the idea of a leader who did not share their own background of culture and ecclesiastical tradition, never entered their thoughts. Moreover, the Master's choice of followers immediately condemned the whole movement in Pharisaic eyes. A cause that numbered a Matthew – a renegade hireling of the foreigner – among its chosen adherents, was obviously not only open to suspicion, it was not even respectable! People whom any sensible Pharisee would quite definitely have discouraged and held at arm's length, were openly welcomed by this indiscriminating Jesus. It almost looked as if he had more interest in the riff-raff of society than in religion's acknowledged leaders! The conclusion was obvious, written as plain as day all over the revival movement the prophet of Galilee had started – the man was an impostor.

Here we see the distinctive Pharisaic sin in action – the sin of scorn. Jesus once told a story which had two characters in it: a Pharisee and a publican. 'God, I thank thee,' said the Pharisee, 'that I am not as other men are' (Luke 18:11). That was the Pharisaic spirit exactly. The sin of the Pharisee was the deadly sin of the superior person. And the worst of that superior feeling was that it came out chiefly in spiritual things: his pride was that most devastating and soul-destroying and godless thing – pride of goodness, pride of grace. Blinded by this complacent sin, eaten up by their own self-righteousness, unable to see God when he came to them through ways not of their own narrow conceiving, they pronounced Jesus an impostor, and planned to hurry him out of the way.

The second element in the conflict between Jesus and the Pharisees was *his attitude to the law and to tradition.* Punctilious observance of all the 613 commandments which made up the Jewish law (and it is significant that of these 613, 365 were negative and 248 positive) was the sum and substance of Pharisaic religion. Orthodoxy declared that these commandments contained the truth, the whole truth, and nothing but the truth. If you had ventured to suggest to a Pharisee that the teachers who had given the law had been dead for years, whereas God was still alive, and that therefore there might conceivably by this time be something to add to it; or if you had hinted to him that a good many of his 613 commandments savoured of an obsolete and pedantic legalism and ought now to be decently buried in order to leave room for new light and truth to come breaking in – he would have held up his hands in horror and called it rank heresy. Jesus took that line, and therefore Jesus was branded a heretic (Mark 2:18, 24). He came challenging men to rethink God: but that, to the tightly-shut mind of a Pharisee, was preposterous and intolerable. It is a startling thought, but it is written plain across the Gospel story, that a great part of the responsibility for the death of Christ at Calvary must be laid at the door of the sin of the closed mind. 'Surely,' said George Meredith, 'an unteachable spirit is one of the most tragic things in life.' It is, indeed. It was an unteachable spirit that erected the Cross.

This aspect of the matter deserves to be emphasised. In every department of life and thought, Jesus is on the side of the open, hospitable mind which welcomes new truth gladly. 'The Lord,' said John Robinson, the pastor of the Pilgrim Fathers, 'hath more truth yet to bring forth from his word.' Unfortunately, history abounds in illustrations of Bertrand Russell's saying that 'men fear thought as they fear nothing else on earth'; and nearly every new truth which has won its way in the world has had to begin by fighting for its very life against the determined opposition of those who should have welcomed it. But Jesus stands for absolute honesty of every kind, including intellectual honesty. 'I am the truth,' he said (John 14:6). And therefore the obscurantist spirit, the closed mind in every form, is fundamentally irreligious. How ignoble that spirit is revealed once and for all on the day when it helped to crucify the Lord of glory.

The third charge in the Pharisaic indictment of Jesus concerned his *universalism.* To the average Pharisee, mankind fell into two groups: one composed of true-born Jews, the other containing all the rest, called indiscriminately and contemptuously 'Gentiles'. There was an insurmountable barrier between them. The very name Pharisee meant 'separated'. Judaism had a monopoly of the true religion. The Jew had vested rights in God. This was the spirit to which Jesus flung down the gauntlet. God, he declared, was everywhere, and for everybody. Despised Samaritans were no less God's children than people born and bred in Jerusalem (Luke 10:30ff; John 4:4ff). Of a Roman soldier, he said, 'I have not found so great faith, no, not in Israel' (Matthew 8:10). He drew a picture of a day when all the roads of the world would be filled with marching hosts, people out of every nation under heaven streaming up to the Kingdom of God (Luke 13:29). This universalism struck at everything the exclusive Pharisee held sacred and most dear: it was dangerous doctrine, and the man who proclaimed it must be silenced.

3 *The* OPPOSITION *of the* SADDUCEES

Along these different lines the opposition of the Pharisees developed. But they did not stand alone. The Sadducees joined hands with them. Between Pharisee and Sadducee there had often been strain and tension, and sometimes open strife: but common hostility to Jesus bridged the gulf, and made them friends for once. Three things have to be kept in mind in thinking about the Sadducees. They were an *aristocratic* party, containing members of the old nobility. They were a *political* party, controlling the nation's interests at home and abroad. They were a *priestly* party, holding the leading places in the Sanhedrin. The Sadducean spirit was marked by a crass materialism and worldliness. Their outlook on life was utterly secular. Recognising that their own position depended on maintaining the existing order of things, they adopted towards all new movements, alike in Church and State, an attitude defiantly reactionary. Religion was made subservient to politics. What religion they had was largely of a negative kind, consisting in a denial of certain doctrines which their Pharisaic opponents embraced. They accepted the Jewish law, but denied the accumulated 'tradition' which generations of scribes and Pharisees had added to it. They denied the Messianic hope. They denied the resurrection of the dead and the belief in personal immortality.

It was almost inevitable that the Sadducean spirit and the spirit of Jesus should come sooner or later into open conflict. To this worldly-minded priestly aristocracy, Jesus was definitely a dangerous person: they felt insecure as long as he was at liberty. The danger was not only that his teaching might precipitate a nation-wide movement, which would lead to a clash with Rome, with disastrous consequences to the established political order and to their own comfortable position. There was the further danger which a living religion always occasions to a dead religion. The word of God in Jesus' mouth was like a sword, piercing through shows and shams and unreality. It blazed with honesty. It made insincerity tremble. It was alive, incalculable, life-changing, revolutionary. Hence the Sadducees detested it. They detested even more the man who proclaimed it. They would have no peace, they told themselves, until the word was silent and the man dead.

4 *The* OPPOSITION *of the* CROWD

Another factor now entered into the situation. There came a point in Jesus' ministry when many of the common people turned against him. The enormous popularity of earlier days began to wane, and the ranks of his admirers and friends sadly thinned. How do we explain this change in popular sentiment?

Disappointed hopes partly accounted for it. Seeing Jesus' mighty works, and listening to his authoritative words, many of the people had begun to feel that here was the very Captain they were needing to lead them in their next revolt and insurrection against the Roman power. And it annoyed them to see him apparently squandering his opportunities. It angered them that he should lose time and be so irritatingly unpractical when he might have been giving reality to their hopes by smiting a passage for himself to the throne. Once, indeed, they came to take him by force and make him a king (John 6:15). At the very last, the hopes that had been smothered flared up again in the great Palm Sunday demonstration (Matthew 21:8ff). There can be no doubt that Jesus' steadfast refusal to fall in with the demand for a national leader turned a great mass of potential support into open hostility.

Another factor was *the success of the Pharisees in poisoning the popular mind.* The Pharisees deliberately set themselves to sow suspicions of Jesus everywhere. The Galilean ministry had scarcely begun when delegates were sent north from Jerusalem for this purpose (Mark 3:22). Wherever in the story of these Galilean days any traces of opposition appear, sinister figures are in the background fanning the sparks into a flame (Mark 2:6; 7:1). Now the Pharisees were the accredited religious leaders of the nation, and their work of spreading damaging rumours about Jesus naturally had a huge effect upon people who were easily led. It would have been a simple matter for Jesus, if he had so chosen, to counter them with their own weapons; but Jesus would use no weapons but God's, and so the subtle, unholy influence went on. The poison did its work.

But apart from such causes, many people were alienated by *the Gospel Jesus preached and the demands he made.* It was no comfortable Gospel. His demands were imperious. To the natural man, the Sermon on the Mount, if taken seriously, was an utterly impracticable programme, and the Master who proclaimed it an impossible person. A religion which claimed, as the religion of Jesus did, a full and unconditional surrender, could never be 'popular' in the accepted sense of the word. Jesus always told people bluntly that the gate was strait (Matthew 7:14). Love to one's enemies, forgiveness unto seventy times seven – these were the radical, overwhelming tests he dared to apply (Matthew 5:44; 18:22). No half-measures were to be allowed. 'If thy right hand offend thee,' he said 'cut it off' (Matthew 5:30).

Discipleship of Jesus, on these terms, was obviously an affair for heroes. It still is, and always will be, a heroic thing – a fact which has often been blurred and forgotten because his own followers have failed to take him seriously, and have been content to acknowledge him without facing up to his demand for a full surrender. In Galilean days, the stringency of the Master's demand soon chilled the enthusiasm of many who had once given him a rapturous welcome; and it was of these that he was thinking when, in one of his greatest parables, he spoke about the seed in stony places which springs up quickly and gives real promise, but ere long withers away (Matthew 13:5f). The very Gospel Jesus preached turned many from friends to foes. For a world ordered on a selfish basis will never be able to do anything with God but crucify him.

5 *The* HERO CHRIST

So the shadows deepened and the storm gathered. Jesus knew that the hour for which God had appointed him could not now be far away. He determined on a bold stroke. He would meet the opposition at its headquarters. He would carry the campaign up to the capital. There in the city of God the final revelation must be given, the decisive blow struck at the powers of darkness, and the uttermost sacrifice of redeeming love accepted. 'He steadfastly set his face to go to Jerusalem' (Luke 9:51).

From this point on, one steady, dazzling flame can be seen burning through the shadows as they deepened into midnight – the heroism of the soul of Jesus. Listen to his words: 'I have a baptism to be baptised with; and how am I straitened till it be accomplished!' (Luke 12:50). 'I must walk today, and tomorrow, and the day following: for it cannot be that a prophet perish out of Jerusalem' (Luke 13:33). So with high head and steady eyes and firm step he went, with no weapons but his love, no resources but God and his own indomitable soul, to where the entrenched and embattled forces of evil were waiting for him. No wonder the Evangelist, describing one stage of that last march, has put it like this: 'Jesus went before them: and they were amazed; and as they followed, they were afraid' (Mark 10:32). 'Jesus,' says Bengel finely, 'was dwelling in his passion.'

If evangelical Christianity, emphasising (and rightly) the wonderful tenderness of Jesus, has sometimes obscured the blazing heroism of the Master's soul, here on the road sweeping south out of Galilee towards Jerusalem that heroism must be rediscovered and its overwhelming spell laid on heart and conscience again. And especially today, when a world grown impatient of sentimentalisms and insincerities is beginning to realise that religion is not a mass of shibboleths, but a brave, glad quality of life; when we are learning that the real saints of the Church are not the feeble, ineffective spirits who wail 'Thy will be done' with a sigh of futile resignation, but the people who shout it like a battle-cry – 'Thy will be done!' – and go out to take the kingdom by storm; not those who shun the hard way, but those who tread it with a song – the young man who is living to God in the difficult atmosphere of office or shop or factory or club; the young woman to whom the law of Christ matters more than the law of her social set – in such a day as this, it is a Captain, a Commander, who is needed. Here, on the royal road of the Cross, he stands, the Hero-Christ, a leader for whom people would gladly die. So the strong Son of God went out to his last crusade.

6 The TRANSFIGURATION

Just before he left Galilee, a strange event happened which strengthened Jesus mightily for what lay ahead. Six days after the great self-disclosure at Caesarea Philippi, Jesus took Peter, James and John to Mount Hermon and was transfigured before them (Matthew 17:1ff; Mark 9:2ff; Luke 9:28ff). Shrouded in mystery and difficult to interpret as this wonderful incident must always be, it was certainly no dream or fancy, but a real experience – a spiritual experience of the first order for the three disciples, and an experience of supreme spiritual exultation for their Master. The unseen world, which is after all the most real world, came breaking through while Jesus prayed; and as long before at Dothan a prophet's servant had suddenly caught sight of the horses and chariots of God (II Kings 6:17), so the disciples became aware that spiritual hosts were hovering round their Master and themselves and crowding in to their defence. Dimly we can understand the reinforcing effect upon the soul of Jesus when the voice from Heaven cried, 'My beloved Son'. It was the seal of God's approval set upon Jesus' choice of the Cross. It was the assurance that God had a mighty stake in what was happening now upon the earth, and that behind the shadow and thundercloud and threatening tragedy stood power and love eternal, pledged to crown the soul of Christ with victory.

In that holy hour, there shone out upon the face of Jesus a light which the disciples had never seen before. Our familiar hymn says:

Jesus, these eyes have never seen
That radiant form of Thine;
The veil of sense hangs dark between
Thy blessèd face and mine.

But here on Hermon it was as though that veil of sense had been drawn aside by the hand of God himself, and through the human form of Jesus the very Spirit of the Eternal was revealed – 'We beheld his glory.'

Mystic contemplation, depth of spiritual communion, ecstasy of soul, flooding in from on high – all that entered into the experience of that wonderful hour which made the face of Jesus shine more brightly than any angel's. But there was another element, too, in the Transfiguration, which no careful reader of the Gospels can miss. Here on the Mount, Jesus made a new and final consecration of himself to the will of God his Father. Here he laid his body and soul on the altar of utter sacrifice. Here he surrendered himself to the last dread demand of his vocation as Redeemer. What had been begun at Nazareth, and sealed at the Jordan, and deepened through all the Galilean days, was here on Hermon made complete, when, with a great passion of joy flooding his being, he accepted the Cross. 'Lo, I come to do thy will, O God.'

This does not mean, of course, that Jesus was 'in love with death'. Very different was his spirit from that which speaks in the lines Keats wrote, listening to the nightingale's song:

> *Darkling I listen; and, for many a time*
> *I have been half in love with easeful Death,*
> *Call'd him soft names in many a mused rhyme,*
> *To take into the air my quiet breath;*
> *Now more than ever seems it rich to die.*
> *To cease upon the midnight with no pain.*

There was nothing of that in Jesus. 'In him was *life*,' says St John. He was made for life. He loved life passionately. We do not honour Jesus by imagining that he accepted Calvary easily. He hated death. Death was one of the powers he had come to destroy. But to Jesus, God's will was everything. It was God's will that the world should be redeemed; and if the achievement of that redemption lay on the road of the supreme sacrifice, then – welcome Death! That was Jesus' spirit. He loved life dearly, but he loved God's will far more. And mingling with the ecstasy of the Transfiguration was the joy of an absolute self-consecration, a divine joy whose light in that moment flooded his soul and shone out on his face, and brought his amazed disciples down in adoration at his feet.

Hence from the heart of this mysterious crisis in the life of Jesus, a clear challenge reaches us all. The one thing for which we have been created is the doing of the will of God. Obedience to that will may mean sacrifice, and self-negation, and the hard road of the Cross; but there alone can joy be found, and peace, and a life made radiant and shining like the sun. The road of self-consecration is the King's highway: and we are lost if we are not travelling there.

XVII
The Last Days

1 *The* KING *enters his* CAPITAL

AFTER the crisis of the Transfiguration, Jesus moved on towards the south, preaching and teaching as he went. In many villages of Samaria and Judea lying along the route, he proclaimed his message of the Kingdom and healed the sick; and it was most probably during this time that the mission of his seventy followers took place (Luke 10:1ff). But Jerusalem was his final objective. St Mark's narrative indeed passes straight from the Galilean ministry to the final week in Jerusalem, but considerations of chronology indicate that a whole section of Luke's Gospel (from 9:51 to 18:14) belongs to the interval between. According to St John's account, twice at least before Calvary, Jesus was actually in Jerusalem – at the feast of Tabernacles in October (John 7:2,10), and at the feast of Dedication in December (John 10:22). But it was with the coming of the greatest religious event in the Jewish year – the Passover festival in March – when the Holy City was crowded with throngs of pilgrims from every quarter, that Jesus knew the decisive hour had arrived.

On the Friday evening, six days before the Passover, he reached Bethany. The following day – the Sabbath – was spent in quiet rest, and next morning he prepared to enter Jerusalem. Great companies of pilgrims were flocking in towards the city; and others, hearing that the Galilean prophet, whose fame was now nation-wide, was approaching, came out to line the roads and watch him as he passed. All reserve was now over, and when Jesus entered Jerusalem on that Palm Sunday, he entered it as God's Messiah. That was the meaning of the pageantry of that tumultuous hour, and he openly accepted the tribute. Popularity had waxed and waned, but now for a brief moment it was reborn. Suddenly the flame that had died to a cold ember blazed up again.

Most of the pilgrims acclaiming Jesus with their Hosannas were no doubt provincials, his own countrymen from Galilee in the north – an entirely different crowd from the city rabble which was to cry 'Crucify him' before the week was over. It must not be forgotten that even after the tide of popular sentiment had begun to set against him, and indeed up to the very last, there were thousands of people to whom Jesus remained a friend and a hero – people whom he had healed of bodily diseases, families whose tangled home-life he had straightened out, men and women for whom spiritually he had made all things new. They brought their tribute to him now. Amid the shouts of the welcoming throng, the king rode towards his capital. 'Blessed is he that cometh in the name of the Lord!'

By this act Jesus declared himself. No longer, as at the beginning of his ministry, did he withdraw from the plaudits of the crowd. No longer, as in Galilean days, did he hold back the secret of his royal dignity from all save the initiated few. Ringing in his mind were the words of one of the great prophets of his people, words which often from his boyhood days he had pondered – 'Rejoice greatly, O daughter of Zion; shout, O daughter of Jerusalem: behold, thy King cometh unto thee' (Zechariah 9:9). At last the old seer's dream had come true. Not for ever should the daughter of Zion have to wait for her Lover and her Lord. Not for ever should the throne of David stand vacant. By his action on that Palm Sunday, Jesus said in a way more plain than words, 'Behold your King!'

The entrance into Jerusalem was an acted parable. It gave the faithful the sign they had been waiting for. It inaugurated the Master's final mission to his people, and was a fitting prelude to the days of intense activity and emotion which were to follow. It focused the whole city's attention on Jesus, so that, wherever he went during that closing week, crowds followed him, and his name was on every tongue. And, most important, it flung down the gauntlet to his enemies. It defied them. Much they could endure, but this procession through the streets was intolerable. This fanatic and usurper must be put down finally. Jesus in that tumultuous hour was issuing a challenge. Every token of royal honour which he accepted that day gave point to the challenge, and every Hosanna of the crowd drove it home. Let the powers of evil do their worst: he knew his power. He was the Lord's Anointed. He was riding to the throne which God had given him. He was ready for the last campaign.

But even then, lest the excitement of the hour might revive in the breasts of the crowd those material and national ideas of Messiahship and kingship which were so foreign to his mind, Jesus did something to make it clear that his was no earthly monarchy, but an empire of the spirit – he would have no proudly caparisoned war-horse to carry him, but only an ass's colt. 'Behold, thy King cometh unto thee, meek, and sitting upon an ass, and a colt the foal of an ass' (Matthew 21:5).

Moreover, something which happened as the procession moved slowly towards the city must have puzzled and startled any who were imagining that in Jesus they had found another Maccabaeus. Where the winding road crept round the shoulder of Olivet, the city suddenly came into view; and Jesus halted (Luke 19:41ff). They saw him sitting silent and absorbed. They saw him gazing at the city spread out before him. And then – to their amazement – they saw tears in the eyes that gazed. Jesus wept! They did not know the reason for those tears. They did not understand how his heart was aching for the stubbornness, the blindness, of the city that he loved. They did not realise how he was foreseeing the day, so soon to come, when fire and sword would seal Jerusalem's fate. They only knew that the Leader, whom they had hoped to see asserting himself with martial vigour and remorseless might, was weeping. And they wondered. And they were disquieted. When the procession was formed again and moved on, the Hosannas were perhaps a little less convinced. Was this, after all, the King they had expected? But Christ's thoughts were not their thoughts; and when the day was over, and excitement still ran high, he slipped away, to the bitter disappointment and chagrin of those who still hankered after a Messiah who would take the throne by force, and returned quietly to Bethany.

2 *The* SHADOWS *deepen*

On the next two days, Monday and Tuesday, Jesus was again in the city. Fearlessly and without any attempt at concealment, he showed what he thought of the unholy traffic that was desecrating his Father's house (Matthew 21:12f). Never did the volcanic element in the soul of Christ blaze out more terribly than in the hour when he stood in the Temple courts with the whip of cords raised above his head, and in his eyes a light before which strong men quailed and a whole jostling multitude was cowed to silence and shrank away. To those days belong also the public controversies with his opponents, notably the discussion on the tribute money (which we have examined in some detail already), and the terrific onslaught on Pharisaic casuistry and hypocrisy (Matthew 23) which made the breach complete and sealed his doom.

Two days before the Passover, a meeting of the Sanhedrin was hastily convened to discuss ways and means of suppressing Jesus finally. The Sanhedrin was an aristocratic body, 71 in number, forming the General Council of the Jewish nation and also the High Court of Justice. It consisted of chief priests and scribes and elders. As its membership included leaders both of the Pharisees and of the Sadducees, friction and strife often marked its deliberations; but in the matter of Jesus a concordat seems to have been reached, and both parties were united in demanding his arrest.

How to carry out that arrest was the dilemma. The real difficulty was the mercurial temperament of the crowd. No one knew with certainty whether an open, official move by the Sanhedrin would precipitate a sudden revulsion of popular feeling in favour of Jesus – an awkward problem, demanding careful strategy. But an entirely unexpected solution offered itself when one of the Master's own followers craved an audience of the Court. The man was ushered in. Jesus, he said, could be taken secretly, under cover of darkness. He himself knew his Master's movements in advance. He knew his favourite haunts. He would lead them there, and they would have Jesus at their mercy. So the ugly, treacherous scheme was unfolded. Blood money was given, and the pact was sealed (Matthew 26:14ff).

3 *The* UPPER ROOM

The Wednesday of that week seems to have been spent by Jesus in seclusion, either in Bethany or among the hills. But on the Thursday evening, at the hour of the Paschal feast, Jesus sat down with his disciples in the guest-chamber of one of his nameless friends in Jerusalem. Only a brief hour or two now, and the storm would break in devastating fury; but here in this quiet upper room the very peace of God was reigning. Here the great Christian Sacrament of all the ages was instituted. Here the deathless words about the home of many mansions were spoken, and the promise of the Comforter was given. And here the Master ate and drank for the last time before he died, with the men whom God had given him out of the world – the faithful few who, through sunshine and cloud, had clung to him and companied with him down the years and loved him tonight most passionately. Here Jesus trysted them to meet him again and to receive from his hands another cup at the banquet of God in heaven.

It is small wonder that this upper room has been a dearer place to Christendom than all the great cathedrals raised by subsequent ages to Jesus' honour. Its story was not finished when the Master rose from the table there and led his friends out to Gethsemane; it was not finished when the candles were extinguished that night and silence reigned again. For when after Calvary the broken-hearted, leaderless disciples sought a hiding-place and refuge from the threatening mob, it was in this same upper room that they found it. This was the place which witnessed their hopeless mourning for the Master they had lost, and this was the place where that mourning was turned to bewildered, incredulous joy when Jesus came back to them through the closed and bolted door, and revealed himself risen and alive (John 20:19). Here, too, it is more than likely, they gathered again when he had ascended to his Father; and here the Spirit fell, flooding their souls with the glory of Pentecost, and giving birth to the Christian Church (Acts 1:13; 2:1).

If the tradition is correct which identifies this upper room with the house in Jerusalem to which Peter made his way on his escape from prison (Acts 12:12), we should be able to conclude that the 'goodman of the house' who figures so mysteriously in the Gospel story (Mark 14:14), was none other than the husband of Mary, the mother of John Mark, the earliest Evangelist. We saw earlier (see chapter I, 'The Gospel records') that the 'certain young man' who, according to Mark's Gospel, was present in Gethsemane and escaped with difficulty when Jesus was arrested, may have been Mark himself (Mark 14:51). We can imagine him helping his father and mother to prepare the upper room for Jesus and his friends, waiting outside the door while the Last Supper was celebrated that night, and then following the little group out to the garden on Olivet to see what was to happen. Be that as it may, this upper room of many memories will always draw and hold the hearts of Christ's people wherever the Gospel is preached; and every time the bread of our Communion is broken and the wine poured out, we feel that we are meeting with Jesus there.

'This do in remembrance of me,' said Jesus (Luke 22:19). It was the Lord's last wish, and Christendom has always held it sacred. In the simple, yet unfathomably profound, action of the Lord's Supper, faith has been nourished down the centuries, and hope kindled, and love sustained. Three kinds of language are at our disposal when we seek to communicate the thoughts of our hearts. There is *the language of words*: but we all know how soon this breaks down, and how difficult it is to find any words to carry the deepest things. Beyond the language of words, there is *the language of art* – including music, painting, sculpture – and this, too, religion needs: but here again there is a limit, where the language of art breaks down. Beyond this point, there remains *the language of action*: and this alone can convey life's final sanctities. So the Church, at Christ's command, takes the bread, and breaks it, and sees Calvary before its eyes; takes the wine, and pours it out, and remembers the blood of the Cross by which the world is saved.

We cannot dwell further here on the meaning of the Sacrament which Jesus instituted in the upper room on the night of his betrayal. Suffice to say, the Church, in celebrating the Lord's Supper, has always found – and rightly – not only a *memorial,* but a *presence.* It is not we who do anything in the Sacrament. It is God who comes to us in Christ, and makes himself real to our faith, and blesses us with his cleansing fellowship. 'Here, O my Lord, I see thee face to face.'

4 GETHSEMANE

When midnight came, Jesus rose from the table in the upper room, and led his disciples out to Gethsemane (Matthew 26:36ff). Lying at the foot of the Mount of Olives, it was one of the Master's favourite resorts; this was not the first time they had retired there together for prayer and quiet. But tonight, leaving most of the disciples at the edge of the wood, asking even Peter and James and John to stay a little distance away – for the burden on his soul was now too heavy to be shared even with those who knew him best, and his spirit craved for solitude and God – Jesus went forward to pray alone in the dark. He fell upon his knees. He fell upon his face. He lay with his face to the ground. And then – the agony which none may ever comprehend began: 'O my Father, if it be possible, let this cup pass from me!'

We need not think to fathom the soul of Christ while that agony lasted. Only irreverence would probe for explanations here. But of one thing we may be certain: it was not fear of death that made Jesus shrink. Many martyrs have faced the last hour unflinching, with a song upon their lips – and Jesus was braver than them all. It was not death that made him cry to God: it was sin. It was the shame of all the world, the burden of all the sons of men, which in that dread hour he was taking upon his own sinless heart. It was the sudden sense of sin's sheer horror and loathsomeness and Godforsakenness. It was, as St Paul with characteristic daring expressed it, one who 'knew no sin' being 'made sin' for men (II Corinthians 5:21). Deeper than this we dare not seek to go. If Christ in his agony left even 'the beloved disciple' behind, it is not for us to intrude. We can only stand afar off, and hear the cry out of the darkness – 'O God, let this cup pass!' But then, listening still, we hear another cry breaking the silence, a prayer calm and resolute and full of the peace of a great acceptance – 'O my Father, if this cup may

not pass away from me, except I drink it, thy will be done'
(Matthew 26:42). So the faith which never once throughout
his life had wavered, remained victor even here.

By this time the disciples, weary in body and mind with
the strain of these last days, had fallen asleep. Had they been
awake and watchful, they might have seen the lights of torches
flickering on the edge of the wood. They might have seen dim
figures moving among the trees. But there was none keeping
guard. In any case, resistance by force was far from Jesus'
thoughts; and when Judas and the Temple police and their
attendant rabble came, they found little difficulty in effecting
the arrest. The Master was led away, and the disciples, having
lost their nerve completely now, 'all forsook him and fled'
(Matthew 26:56).

5 *The* ENIGMA *of* JUDAS

Before passing to the subsequent events of that night of treachery, we must pause here and consider the man who played the
traitor. That one who had been in Jesus' company from the
first, living daily under the spell and influence of the gracious
presence of the Son of God, should have fallen into this appalling
infamy at the end, has seemed to some students of Scripture
so utterly incomprehensible that they have been driven to the
conclusion that this was no ordinary man at all, but Satan
incarnate, a monster in human disguise. Such a reading of the
enigma, however, is unsatisfactory: it does justice neither to the
point of view of the Evangelists, nor to the facts of psychology.
We must probe deeper.

There had been a day when Judas, like Peter and Andrew and
the rest, had left all to follow Christ. That is a fact of cardinal
importance. He forsook home and kindred for Jesus' sake.
No doubt hopes of an earthly kingdom played a part in that

decision; but over and above these was the fact that the man felt the magnetism of Jesus. The appeal of the young Prophet from Galilee moved him as nothing else had ever moved him in his life before; and when the call came, it found him ready.

Even more important is the fact of Jesus' estimate of Judas. The Master's eye, accustomed to reading all kinds of men, detected in Judas the makings of a real apostle; here was a man who had it in him to do splendid service for the Kingdom. Sometimes, indeed, it has been suggested that Jesus gave Judas a place near himself simply because it was necessary for God's predestined plans that there should be a traitor in the disciple band. It cannot be too strongly insisted that any such theory is both absurd and irreligious. It turns predestination into fatalism. It is a slander on Providence and on God's ordering of the world. It degrades the sacred narrative to the level of solemn play-acting. No, Jesus called Judas to be a disciple for the same reason for which he called the other eleven. He saw in him a man of noble promise and boundless possibilities. No doubt he saw other things as well – moral contradictions jostling one another in the man's secret soul, strange conflicts of light and darkness, courage and cowardice, self-surrender and self-love. But that simply meant that he was a man of human passions; and it was out of such materials that Jesus fashioned his saints. He hoped to do it here. Judas, when he first became a disciple, was a potential man of God.

To begin with, all went well. He was out on the great adventure of his life, and he knew it. But gradually a subtle change came over him. It was as if the spring had gone out of the year. He was less comfortable with his Master now than formerly. The other disciples may never have noticed that anything was happening, but Jesus did. Jesus' secret midnight prayers at this period must have been burdened with Judas's name. The change in the man's attitude seems to have been a direct outcome of Jesus' constant endeavour to spiritualise his followers' earthly and material Messianic hopes and of his failure to take the tide of popularity at the flood. To Judas, such dilatory and unpractical ways were inexplicable and unpardonable: the flood-tide might have led them all on to fortune and spectacular success, but now the chance was lost for ever, deliberately thrown away, and his heart was sore and aggrieved and turning bitter.

This suggests the real motive of his foul deed of treachery. Various motives have been canvassed. *Was it love of money?* That there was a streak of covetousness in his nature is pretty certain, and he seems to have indulged in petty pilfering. One of the Evangelists says bluntly that he was a thief (John 12:6). But it is hard to believe that money was the master-passion for which he sold his Lord. He could so easily have driven a better bargain with the priests, if that had been his object! The thirty pieces of silver might have been doubled or trebled.

Was jealousy the motive? This may have played a part. The fact that he was the only Judean among the Twelve, all the rest being Galileans (Iscariot means 'the man from Kerioth', a village of Judea) may have tended to make him solitary, aloof and critical; and we can well believe that, to a man of his ambitious nature, Jesus' choice of Peter, James and John to form the inner circle of the disciple group (Mark 5:37; 9:2) must have rankled. But jealousy alone will not explain his crime.

Another theory suggests *fear as the motive.* According to this, Judas saw disaster impending, and realised that when the crash came it would involve not only the Leader of the cause, but all his followers as well: when Jesus went down, he would drag the rest down with him. The frightened disciple saw that the only way to secure himself and save his own skin, when the worst came to the worst, was to turn king's evidence, in the hope that the authorities, grateful for the help he had given them to lay hands upon their main enemy, would let the informer go free. Certainly we cannot rule this motive out. Yet it does not cover all the facts.

De Quincey made the famous suggestion that Judas played the traitor *in order to force Jesus' hand*. Writhing with impatience as he watched his Master apparently squandering one opportunity after another of asserting himself and claiming the throne, Judas at last decided that if Jesus would not take action of his own accord, he would have to be compelled to act. But how? Obviously the way to do it would be to get Jesus into a compromising situation. Then he would be forced to bestir himself and manifest his power. Then the kingdom would come. It is an ingenious theory, and, if accepted, it would go far to rehabilitate the worst reputation in history. But it will not hold water. It represents Jesus as an irresolute, procrastinating Hamlet. Instead of Judas the traitor, it gives us Judas the misguided saint. Instead of a deep-dyed crime, it speaks of an error of judgement. There is not a scrap of evidence for this in the Gospels. It is quite inconsistent with the words of stern condemnation which Jesus himself used about his disciple's deed. An error of judgement, the rashness of a too enthusiastic follower, Jesus would certainly have pardoned. But of Judas he could only say – 'Woe to that man by whom the Son of man is betrayed! good were it for that man if he had never been born' (Mark 14:21). No, this explanation must be set aside.

We are left with what was almost certainly the real motive – *the man's bitter, revengeful spirit*. Disappointment of his worldly hopes bred spite, and spite deepened into hatred. Judas kept telling himself that he had been deceived, led on by false pretenses, that these years of his life had been wasted, and that all Jesus had done for him had been to land him in desperate trouble; well, he would strike back! He would have his revenge. Besides, he had known for long that the steady eyes of Jesus were reading him like a book, discovering all his secret insincerities of thought and character. Jesus, he knew, saw right through him. That intensified the man's anger and vindictiveness. He began to toy with the thought of treachery. Once that thought had found a lodging in his mind, the rest of the tempter's task was easy. Soon the thought had become a fixed idea, and the deterioration of his soul was startling in its rapidity. Nothing could save him now, not even the sight of Jesus kneeling before him to wash his feet (John 13:5), not the final appeal of Jesus at the supper table (John 13:26). By that time, he had sold his soul irretrievably. Only the deed itself now remained. But what evil spirit suggested the signal he arranged with his accomplices that night? It was the crowning touch of horror, the last point of infamy beyond which human infamy could not go, when out in the garden Judas betrayed his Master, not with a shout or a blow or a stab, but with a kiss.

XVIII
Jesus on Trial

1 *The* DOUBLE TRIAL

To understand what happened between Gethsemane and Calvary, we must try to grasp quite clearly the reason why Jesus was subjected to a double trial. We call it a trial; in reality it was an inquisition; the death sentence, when it was carried out, was nothing more or less than judicial murder.

Jesus appeared first before the Jewish Sanhedrin: this was the ecclesiastical trial. Then he was sent to a Roman tribunal: this was the civil trial. Had the charge on which Jesus appeared not been a capital one, the Sanhedrin alone could have decided the matter, without referring to Pilate at all. For in Judea, as in all the provinces of her far-flung empire, Rome gave the conquered people a fair measure of self-government; and the judicious application of this Home Rule principle contributed largely to the maintenance of peace throughout her dominions. But where death sentences were involved, as in the case of Jesus, Rome reserved the final right of judgement for herself. Such cases, after going through the Jewish court, had to come up again for review before the Roman authorities, who had the power either to homologate the verdict already pronounced and execute sentence on the accused, or to overturn the proceedings altogether and set the prisoner free. This explains what happened on the night of Christ's arrest.

2 JESUS *before* ANNAS

The Temple police who arrested him in Gethsemane took Jesus first to Annas (John 18:13). Now this part of the proceedings was, strictly speaking, quite informal and arbitrary. Annas held no official position. But he wielded an immense influence and prestige, and in the Sanhedrin no man's opinion carried greater weight. Twenty years before, he had been high priest, a title which he still received by courtesy; and no fewer than five of his sons had succeeded him in this, the highest position in the land. It is probable that it was Annas who had established, for reasons of personal gain, the traffic of the bazaar within the Temple courts which Jesus had so sternly denounced. He was the evil genius behind the plots that had led to Jesus' capture; and though it was after midnight when the prisoner was brought in, the old man was alert and wakeful and determined to push the case forward without delay. After an informal preliminary inquiry, he sent Jesus on to Caiaphas.

3 JESUS *before* CAIAPHAS

Caiaphas, Annas' son-in-law, was high priest and head of the Sanhedrin. He was the accredited guardian of the nation's soul, set apart to be the supreme interpreter and representative of the Most High. To him was committed the glorious privilege of entering once every year into the Holy of Holies. Yet this was the man who condemned the Son of God. History provides no better illustration of the truth that the best religious opportunities in the world, and the most promising environment, will not guarantee a man's salvation or of themselves ennoble his soul. 'Then I say,' says John Bunyan, closing his book, 'that there was a way to hell, even from the gates of heaven.'

News of Jesus' arrest had by this time been carried round,

and had brought many members of the Sanhedrin to the high priest's house. According to its constitution, the Sanhedrin could not legally be convened before the hour of sunrise; but Caiaphas and the rest were impatient, and decided to proceed with the examination of the prisoner at once. All that would then remain for the formal meeting after sunrise would be the ratification of any decisions arrived at meanwhile at the informal sitting, and valuable time would thus be saved (Matthew 26:57; 27:1).

Caiaphas began by putting questions to Jesus about his disciples and his doctrine (John 18:19). No doubt he hoped to draw from Jesus some statement of his teaching which could be twisted round to mean that he had anti-Roman sympathies: this could then be used decisively against him when the trial before the Roman governor began. But this first line of attack failed. 'You know my teaching,' said Jesus in effect. 'I have never made any secret of my beliefs: they are public property. Why ask me now?' Caiaphas was discomfited (John 18:20).

Equally unsuccessful was his second attempt. He brought in witnesses against the prisoner, in the hope that they would produce evidence on which, without more ado, sentence of condemnation could be passed. But the witnesses failed to agree, and in any case their evidence was flimsy. Again the President of the Sanhedrin had to own himself balked (Mark 14:56, 59).

Growing anxious and uneasy at the course the investigation was taking, and at the complete failure of the court to substantiate any charge against the accused, Caiaphas suddenly decided to bring his last and most dangerous weapon into action. Point-blank he demanded of Jesus whether he claimed to be Messiah. Now or never, Jesus would incriminate himself! And when Jesus quietly replied, 'I am', adding significantly that a day was coming when the Son of Man would be seen sitting on the right hand of power, the high priest, overjoyed and triumphant that his enemy had given himself away at last, playing into his accusers' hands, cried out that it was blasphemy. No further witnesses were needed, for the prisoner stood condemned out of his own mouth (Mark 14:63f). With this the court unanimously concurred, and the death penalty was decreed.

To all intents and purposes the Jewish trial was over. Formal ratification of the verdict when the Sanhedrin met officially after sunrise would be a matter of a few minutes. Meanwhile the condemned man could be handed over to the tender mercies of his gaolers and the mob. Even members of the court took part in the unholy display of cruelty that followed (Mark 14:65).

It was while this infamy was being perpetrated that there occurred an incident which all four Evangelists record, and which the conscience of the Christian Church has never been able to forget – Simon Peter's denial. Impetuous and devoted to the last, Peter had found his way into the high priest's courtyard. But he had not been there long when he began to rue it. He had an uneasy feeling that he was being watched. There were eyes following him. The place seemed full of eyes. And when the challenge came, sudden and swift and inescapable, he lost his nerve, and clamoured with an oath that Christ had never meant anything to him at all. Just then the guards marched their prisoner past, and Jesus heard. 'The Lord turned, and looked upon Peter. And Peter remembered' (Luke 22:61). Sorrow and heartbreak and pain unutterable were in that look, and the shamed disciple stumbled out into the night, weeping bitterly. The story of it stands here for all generations of Christians to read and ponder; for human hearts are the same today as they were then, and all disloyalties to the Master just as dark as Peter's tragic failure, and forgiving love as amazing as when Jesus met his friend again beyond Calvary and bade him feed his lambs.

4 ILLEGALITY *of the* TRIAL

Let us turn from the ecclesiastical to the civil trial of Jesus. But let us first summarise the points at which the proceedings thus far had offended against the elementary rules of law and justice. In what respects was the Sanhedrin's judgement illegal?

(1) It was illegal because the court which would decide Jesus' case was an accomplice in his betrayal. Sanhedrin members were inextricably implicated in the secret plots culminating in Judas's treacherous deed. Yet these same men were now to act as jury. This vitiated the proceedings from the outset.

(2) The trial did not begin, as Jewish law demanded, with a statement of a definite charge against the accused. Indeed, the real difficulty of Caiaphas and his friends, as we have seen, was to find any charge at all on which they could commit Jesus to Pilate. When the witnesses disagreed, and no charge was forthcoming, it was the court's duty to abandon the case. This was not done; the proceedings were allowed to drag on. This was illegal.

(3) Moreover, the judge trying the case was also the leader for the prosecution. Caiaphas combined in himself both these roles. He took his place as president of the court that night, absolutely determined in advance to secure a conviction. Had he not already declared, in one of the most cynical and cold-blooded epithets history has preserved for us, that it was 'expedient ... that one man should die for the people' (John 11:50)? When the hearing of witnesses turned out to be a fiasco, the judge himself began putting leading questions to the prisoner. He knew that by doing so he was going against the law, but he would rather have broken the law a hundred times over than let Jesus slip through his fingers now.

(4) Further, there were no witnesses for the defence. None were summoned. None had a chance to appear. It was Jesus against the world. No voice was to be tolerated except the voices of the prosecutors.

(5) But the crowning illegality of the trial was the haste with which it was completed. In the dead of night the case was hurried through. The holding of a brief, formal meeting at

sunrise to ratify the night's work and to give a faint show of legality to what had been done, did not alter the fact that the Sanhedrin's midnight investigation was a flagrant breach of its own laws. But that was not the worst. There was a law that, in capital charges, sentence of death could be pronounced only on the day after the trial: 24 hours had to elapse. There was a further law that such cases were not to be heard at all on the day immediately preceding a Sabbath or one of the great festivals. Both these laws were broken. In their desperate anxiety to get Jesus out of the way before there should be any chance of a popular rising in his favour, his accusers flung principle to the winds and tore justice to shreds.

5 JESUS *before* PILATE

When Caiaphas and his satellites had done their work, Jesus was marched off to the Roman governor for the second stage of his trial. Pontius Pilate had now been procurator for six years, and had found the post by no means a sinecure. The Crown Colony of Judea was one of the most difficult and turbulent corners of Emperor Tiberius's vast dominions. But Pilate's unnecessarily harsh and relentless ways of dealing with the administrative problems that were continually confronting him had made him anything but popular with the people he had to govern. He despised the Jews; he failed altogether to appreciate the religious traditions of their race. No one forgot the day when, in open defiance of Jewish sentiment and in flagrant breach of the conciliatory policy which Rome officially sanctioned, Pilate had caused images of Caesar as god to be carried through the streets of the Holy City. Nor did they forget certain other occasions when he had read the Riot Act and sent his soldiers in amongst the crowds, and caused bloodshed and massacre (Luke 13:1). Neither the Sanhedrin nor the mass of

common people had much love for Pilate; but the spur of necessity works wonders, and it was now the main hope of Caiaphas
and the rest to make a good impression on their governor and
win him to their side, and so secure the death of Jesus.

Pilate began, as was perfectly right, by demanding a definite
statement of the charge (John 18:29). But this was extremely
awkward. For when the Sanhedrin had convicted Jesus, it had
used, as we have seen, the accusation of blasphemy – a purely
religious matter, which was unlikely to carry much weight with
an irreligious Roman, or to be deemed worthy of the death penalty. So the Jews replied evasively. 'If he were not a malefactor,
we would not have delivered him up unto thee' (John 18:30).
Naturally this did not satisfy Pilate, and he pressed for further
information. Whereupon Jesus' accusers, adding yet another
illegality to all that had gone before, quietly dropped the original charge of blasphemy and substituted another in its place,
one of a kind of which Pilate would be bound to take notice –
a charge of treason (Luke 23:2). They declared, first, that Jesus
was perverting the nation (this was a slander); second, that he
forbade paying tribute to Caesar (this was a deliberate untruth
– see Matthew 22:21); and third, that he claimed to be a King
(this was true, though not in the sense which they implied).
Having heard this triple charge, Pilate decided to examine Jesus
in private.

No scene in history has impressed itself more vividly upon
the imagination of the world. Reading between the lines of the
narrative, we begin to see that all through that momentous
hour when the judge was deliberating what to do with this
strange prisoner whom fate had thrown in his way, the prisoner
was wrestling for the soul of his judge. Pilate was not a lost
man yet, and Jesus would fain have saved him from himself.
Moreover, the governor was quick-witted enough to see that
this was no ordinary wrong-doer with whom he had to deal;
he could not but be amazed at the composure and steadiness

and dignity and kingliness of the man in front of him, for whose blood the mob outside was clamouring. He ended the interview, and went forth to declare his verdict – 'Not guilty!'

But this inflamed the passions of the crowd; now, for the first time, fear and uncertainty began to mark Pilate's demeanour. He saw trouble ahead, and became anxious to be rid of this difficult case altogether. In his efforts to evade responsibility, he had recourse to three expedients.

The first was to send Jesus to Herod (Luke 23:7). After all, he argued, Jesus was a Galilean, and therefore subject to Herod's jurisdiction: why should not Herod (who by a great stroke of fortune was in Jerusalem at the time) accept the responsibility and see the trial through to an end? It was clever; but unfortunately for Pilate it did not work out as he had hoped. Back to his palace came the escort with their prisoner a short time later, bearing a message to the effect that Herod thanked the Roman governor for his courtesy, but would not dream of robbing him of his privilege, and begged him to finish the case himself.

The second expedient Pilate tried was a dastardly one. He proposed that, as he could find no fault in Jesus, he would scourge him and release him (Luke 23:16). This sorry compromise was, of course, totally unjustifiable and illogical. It was the poor, fear-driven soul's attempt to do his duty by Jesus and to please the crowd at the same time. But it did neither; and it is no wonder that the angry priests would not accept that verdict at any price. The cries of 'Crucify! Crucify!' grew from a murmur to a tumultuous shout.

Balked in these two attempts, Pilate now tried one last device. He set Jesus over against Barabbas, and gave the crowd their choice, hoping against hope that they would prefer that, of the two, Jesus should live (John 18:39). But this also failed, for there was a loud, acclaiming cry for Barabbas. Pilate was now at his wits' end, when suddenly a voice called out of the crowd, 'If thou let this man go, thou art not Caesar's friend'

(John 19:12). And that settled it. For Pilate knew all too well what that threat meant. The last thing in the world that he wanted was that a complaint against himself should be sent back to his imperial master in Rome. Impeachment would mean ruin, for there were things in his past life which could not bear examination. Anything rather than that! It was his career against Jesus. Well, Jesus would have to go. Gladly as he would have set the man in front of him free, his own interests, his own bad past, blocked the way, and made the sacrifice of innocence essential. He yielded to the clamouring crowd, and sent Jesus to his doom.

6 JESUS *as* JUDGE

So the trial, which was no trial, ended. Let us notice one extraordinary feature of the whole story in closing. Everyone who studies the narratives has the strange feeling that the tables are being turned before his very eyes, and that what he is seeing is not Jesus on trial before Caiaphas or Pilate or Herod: what he is seeing is Caiaphas, Pilate, Herod on trial before Jesus. And when all is over, and the prisoner has been marched away to Golgotha, it is not he who has been judged by them: it is they who have been judged by him. Face to face, each of them – Caiaphas, Pilate, Herod – stood with the Son of Man for a brief hour, and his searchlight played upon their souls, revealing their inmost nature, and showing them up for all the world and for all time to see. On that dark, crowded night, the real Judge was Christ. And where Caiaphas, Pilate and Herod stood that night, every soul at some stage of its life-journey must stand – face to face with Jesus, in the place of decision: and each soul's verdict on the Lord of all good life is, in a deep and solemn sense, Christ's verdict on itself.

XIX
Calvary

1 *The* HOLY *of* HOLIES

WHEN Moses in the desert drew near to the burning bush, he heard a voice bidding him put off his shoes from his feet, for he was standing on holy ground. Our thoughts are to turn now to Calvary, the holiest spot in all the earth, which none dare approach save in the deepest reverence. In this the Gospel writers themselves are our best example. Feeling that here they were handling a theme too high and deep for human words, the Evangelists have given us a narrative marked by noble reticence and perfect restraint. Unutterably poignant and moving their story is, but there is no narrowing of feeling, no working up of emotion: that dignified, reverent reserve characterises it all. Far from diminishing the narrative's power, this quietness and simplicity intensify its effect immeasurably. To take but one example, where in the literature of the world will you find a sentence burdened with a deeper pathos than this – 'Now there stood by the cross of Jesus his mother' (John 19:25)? How restrained and artless that is, for the Evangelist makes no effort to elaborate it; yet, in the picture it conjures up, how overwhelmingly moving! With perfect reverence the Gospels lead us into the holy of holies of our Lord's last hours; and in the writers' simple, unadorned words, all Christendom has found 'thoughts that do often lie too deep for tears'.

2 *A* WILLING SACRIFICE

Jesus, as we have seen in our last two chapters, was put to death by a coalition of definite historic forces. Church and State and people all combined to destroy him. Pharisaic blindness and intolerance, priestly exclusiveness and self-seeking as exemplified in Caiaphas, imperial policy and power as embodied in Pilate, popular disappointment, resentment and revenge as seen in the Jerusalem mob – these were the things which put Jesus on the cross. But it would be a profound mistake to suppose that these historic forces were the final, determining factor. Jesus was not driven to death: he went in the freedom of his own unconquered soul. It was no helpless victim of cruel circumstances who died on Calvary; for in that sacrifice, as the New Testament from first to last insists, Jesus himself was Priest, and willingly laid down his soul upon the altar. 'The Son of Man came,' he said, 'to give his life' (Mark 10:45). And again: 'No man taketh it from me, but I lay it down of myself' (John 10:18).

There was undoubtedly an element of necessity in the death of Jesus: 'The Son of Man,' he said, '*must* suffer, and be slain' (Luke 9:22). But it was necessity not of violence and constraint, but of his own consuming love for mankind. From the beginning Jesus had undertaken his work of world-redemption with his eyes open, knowing full well the price, and willingly accepting it. Hence his amazing calmness and self-possession as the end drew near. Never was fancy further from fact than when his judges imagined themselves masters of the situation at last and controllers of his destiny. Jesus, who from his Galilean days had mastered life, circumstance and every new emergency, was supremely master in that hour when he went, not beaten by human malice or dragged helplessly at the chariot-wheels of fate, but voluntarily and victoriously to the glory of his finished work. This was 'the weakness of God', which 'is stronger than men' (I Corinthians 1:25).

3 *The* OFFENCE *of the* CROSS

Here we should remind ourselves of what death by crucifixion meant in the thoughts of the ancient world. With the passing of the years, Christendom has cast a halo of beauty round the cross. We build our churches in the shape of a cross. We emblazon the cross on the flags of the nations. Beneath the cross we bury our dear dead. We take a Red Cross, and with it symbolise the ministry of healing. Our poets and hymn-writers sing to us of 'the wondrous cross', 'the blessed cross'. But all this ought not to hide from us the fact that originally the cross was a thing unspeakably shameful and degrading. 'Cursed is everyone that hangeth on a tree,' said Paul, quoting Deuteronomy (Galatians 3:13; Deuteronomy 21:23). That was how Jewish feeling expressed it; Roman sentiment was the same. 'This cruellest, most hideous of punishments,' said Cicero, using words in which you can almost hear the shudder – *'crudelissimum taeterrimumque supplicium'*. 'Never may it,' he said elsewhere, 'come near the bodies of Roman citizens, never near their thoughts or eyes or ears!'

Devised in the first instance in semi-barbaric Oriental lands, death by crucifixion was reserved by the Romans for slaves and for criminals of the most abandoned kind. It was a fate of utter ignominy. It was the hangman's rope of the ancient world. Small wonder that when the first Apostles began their world-mission, they found one prejudice everywhere confronting them, among Jews and Gentiles alike – 'the offence, the stumbling-block, of the cross' (Galatians 5:11; I Corinthians 1:23). That the Messiah should die was hard enough to credit; but that he should die *such* a death was utterly beyond belief. Yet so it was. Everything which Christ ever touched – the cross included – he adorned and transfigured and haloed with splendour and beauty; but let us never forget out of what appalling depths he has set the cross on high.

4 *The* CROSS-BEARER

It was the custom of those days, as a refinement of cruelty and a last master-stroke of vindictive insult, to compel a condemned man to carry his own cross to the place of execution. But when the procession to Calvary had been formed and began to move off down the crowd-lined streets, it soon became apparent to the Roman centurion in charge, and to his escort of soldiers, that Jesus would not be able to bear his heavy burden all the way. Exhausted by the frightful scourging to which he had already been subjected (for the iron-tipped thongs of the Roman *flagellum* had done their cruel work all too well), the prisoner sank at last to the ground, and the procession was halted. Now, no Roman would ever have thought of asking another Roman to shoulder a cross, so great were the pollution and the shame of the thing; and therefore the centurion, passing over all his own men, fixed on a stranger standing by and conscripted him for the unwelcome task (Mark 15:21).

A soul's great hour sometimes leaps upon it, and destiny stands waiting all unexpected at the corner of some common road: so it was with Simon of Cyrene, when he turned aside with idle curiosity to watch a passing crowd – before he knew what was happening was carrying the cross of the Son of God. No doubt his first feeling was one of anger and resentment that he had been requisitioned for a duty involving such a stigma. But when, long afterwards, he looked back upon that hour, it was to thank God for the crowning honour of his life. 'The father of Alexander and Rufus,' Mark calls him, obviously referring to two prominent figures of the subsequent apostolic Church (cf Romans 16:13); we cannot escape the conclusion that it was the memory of this hour on the Calvary road, when he took the Master's cross, that changed Simon's life and brought him, and his household with him, to the Christian faith. It is not surprising that the figure of this Cyrenian, appearing so abruptly on history's greatest page, and vanishing again, has fascinated the imagination of Christendom, for among all the services rendered by men and women to Christ in the days of his flesh, this man's service stands alone. Some, like Martha, could spread for him a table. Others, like the good man of the house, could give him sanctuary when foes were near. Others, like the woman who was a sinner, could break their treasures at his feet. But only Simon carried his cross.

5 *The* TITLE *on the* CROSS

When the destination was reached, the soldiers began their work. They laid the cross down upon the ground and stretched their prisoner out upon it, nailing his hands and his feet. Then they lifted it up, and dropped it into the socket in the earth. And then, says Matthew, with one of those vivid touches which say so little but suggest so much, 'sitting down, they watched him there' (Matthew 27:36). They watched him. They were face to face with the event which was to change the world. They were gazing, had they but known it, on God's great heart made bare. They were confronting the very scene to which innumerable souls now owe their ransom. They were in the immediate presence of the final revelation. And they saw – nothing. Gambling and playing with their dice, they whiled the slow hours away. For always there is a moral and spiritual qualification for recognising God.

All the four Evangelists record that over Jesus' head, as he hung dying, there was an inscription. It was common custom, whenever a criminal was executed publicly, to placard the nature of his crime: a brief description of the charge on which the man had been condemned was nailed to the gallows itself, in order that passers-by, looking up and seeing him there, might know what had brought him to that end. Jesus had been condemned because his claims to kingly rights were treasonable and constituted a public danger; and therefore, as the charge and accusation above his head, it stood written, 'Jesus of Nazareth the King of the Jews' (John 19:19).

It was Pilate who chose the wording, and we would like to know what exactly was in his mind. Was the title just a cheap sneer at the carpenter's apprentice whose hallucination had been his ruin; a last fling at the misguided soul who had thought to rival Caesar? Or was it not so much a jest at Jesus' expense as a jest at the expense of the Jews, whom Pilate despised and loved to humiliate – as much as to say, 'This is your king, all the king that poor slaves like you deserve'? That may have been his meaning; for we are told that when the Jewish priests read the inscription, the veiled insult of it so incensed them that they went at once to Pilate and petitioned for its removal. But Pilate only laughed to see them squirming beneath his sarcasm, and retorted, 'What I have written I have written' (John 19:22).

And yet, is it possible that Pilate's meaning went deeper? May it have been that something of Jesus' strength and dignity and innate godlike majesty had laid its spell upon Pilate; that some hint of Jesus' essential royalty, some inkling of the truth of his incredible claim, had dawned upon the procurator's soul; and that it was in obedience to that deep instinct, which he would not have dared to confess even to himself, that he wrote the words, 'This is Jesus the King'?

Be that as it may, we cannot miss the significance of the fact that the inscription was written in three languages, Greek and Latin and Hebrew. No doubt it was done in order to make sure that everyone in the crowd might read it: but Christ's Church has always seen in it – rightly – a symbol of the universal Lordship of her Master. These were the three great world languages, each of them the servant of one dominant idea. Greek was the language of culture and knowledge: in that realm, said the inscription, Jesus was King! Latin was the language of law and government: Jesus was King there! Hebrew was the language of revealed religion: Jesus was King there! Hence, even as he hung dying, truly 'on his head were many crowns' (Revelation 19:12).

6 HIMSELF HE *would not save*

The Tempter who had assailed Jesus in the desert and throughout his life was now to launch his last attack. Members of the Sanhedrin, not content with having secured Christ's condemnation, came out to Calvary to gloat over his sufferings. They began jeering: 'If thou be the Son of God, come down from the cross' (Matthew 27:40). It was not only a taunt: it was a temptation. It was a double temptation. It was a temptation to leave the last dregs of the bitter cup of suffering untasted, to escape before the uttermost farthing of the price of sin was paid. But it was more: it was a temptation to do something dazzling and dramatic at this eleventh hour to compel mankind to believe. 'Let him come down from the cross, *and we will believe*,' cried the crowd. That was the real sting of it for Jesus, for the creating of belief was the aim and object of his life. But now in dying he flung that last temptation from him, and refused the startling miracle: back in the desert he had settled it once and for all that his Kingdom would not come by such spectacular ways (see chapter V, 'The Desert'). And when in bitter mockery they cried, 'He saved others, himself he cannot save' (Matthew 27:42), they were saying something deeper and truer than they knew. It was a fact, indeed the central fact of the Gospel, that in his passion to save the world by giving the final revelation of love, Jesus would not and could not save himself. Not by the Roman nails through his hands, but by the perfect love in his own heart, he was bound to the Cross, bound fast until the work was done; and his refusal to save himself has become the saving of the world.

7 *The* DYING THIEF

Jesus did not die alone. It may have been a desire on the part of his enemies to carry their jests and insults still further which prompted them to hang a thief on either side of him; but though they did not understand it, there was a singular appropriateness in the act. All his life Jesus had been the friend of sinners, and in his death he was not divided from them. God himself, when he had first called his Son to be the Saviour of the world, had indissolubly linked together the love of Jesus and the shame of perishing souls: and what God hath joined together, let not man put asunder.

So to the right and left of Jesus' cross on Calvary the crosses of the two malefactors stood (Luke 23:33). Who were they – these two nameless souls who have thus been thrust into the gaze of centuries? Desperadoes perhaps, like those who (as Jesus' own story of the Good Samaritan reminds us) infested the Jerusalem to Jericho road. It is possible that they were associates of Barabbas the insurrectionist; the revolutionary movement which he headed, though in its beginnings directed with nationalist fervour against the Roman domination, had degenerated into mere brigandage and crime and murder.

Crucified alongside Jesus, both the dying thieves began reviling him. But something about the man on the centre cross brought one of them to silence. This man who had endured and was enduring the frightful agony without a cry, whose bearing even under the shadow of death had something in it strangely royal, who had been praying for the men who drove the nails in, 'Father, forgive them, for they know not what they do' – who could he be? Again and again the thief turned his head to gaze upon that serene and loving face. Who *must* he be? Suddenly, out of the depths, faith rose and stormed the heights. 'Lord, remember me when thou comest into thy kingdom!' (Luke 23:42). It is an amazing tribute to the sheer kingliness of Christ that, at the very last, when everything to outward appearance was lost, and pomp and circumstance were nowhere, one man, gazing at him as death came hurrying on, felt instinctively that he was marching to a throne. 'Verily,' said Jesus, in reply, 'today shalt thou be with me in Paradise', thereby setting the final seal to the truth which he had given his life to declare – that in a single moment, from the dust-heaps and cinder-heaps of life, any ruined hopeless soul, bound in affliction and iron, may pass straight to the perfect release of forgiveness and wear the white robes of a saint.

8 *The* SWELLING *of* JORDAN

There was one moment during these last hours of agony when even the soul of Jesus trembled, for the Father seemed to have hidden his face. We can never hope fully to comprehend what Jesus' thoughts and feelings were when the cry rang out, 'My God, my God, why hast thou forsaken me?' (Matthew 27:46; cf Psalms 22:1). We may say that this dark, mysterious moment was the culmination of his life-long self-identification with men in all the most desolating experiences of their souls: but it was more. We may say that here the unspeakable shame and sickening horror of all the sins of all the sons of men came down overwhelmingly on his own sinless heart: but even that does not fathom the depths of his bitter cry. We can only stand afar off and bow our heads, and leave Christ to traverse that darkness alone. One thing is gloriously certain, that when he reached that breaking-point of faith, his faith refused to break; for when the cry stabbed the silence, it was 'my God, my God' still.

Beyond that cry there came another, like a victor's shout this time, 'It is finished!' (John 19:30). That, indeed, was no more than what everyone else on Calvary was saying then – but with what a difference! It was finished for the soldiers, and they could go back to their barracks now. It was finished for his mother and Mary Magdalene, and the poor remnant who had loved him to the end, and they could go wearily back to a world that would never be the same. It was finished for the jesting priests and the rabble mob, and they could congratulate themselves that their vengeance was complete. But when the man on the centre cross suddenly raised his resolute eyes to the sky, and cried with his dying breath, 'It is finished!', the whole kingdom of darkness must have trembled to its foundations. For it was not only the long strain of life, with its turbulent close, that was finished now for Jesus; nor was this a mere sigh of relief. The work was finished, Satan's empire was finished, the redeeming of the earth was finished; and this was a triumphant assertion of achievement, this was a conquering shout. With that glad cry the soul of Jesus burst home into his Father's presence. He had glorified God on the earth; he had finished the work which God had given him to do.

9 *what the* CROSS *means for the* WORLD

Standing on the holy ground of Calvary today, with eyes raised to the cross, we understand why the conscience of mankind for nineteen centuries has been drawn to this one scene as by a magnet. And why Christians have always felt that the heart of everything lies here. Jesus himself knew and openly affirmed that by his death there would be let loose in the earth a saving, cleansing power beyond all calculation. That power has gone to work mainly along two lines.

On the one hand, the death of Jesus has *revealed sin in its true nature.* Let us remember that the evil things which put Jesus on the cross were by no means unfamiliar or abnormal. Self-interest in Caiaphas, fear in Pilate, impurity in Herod, anger and spite in the crowd – these were the things which, coming in contact with the Sinless One, deliberately compassed his death.

That is to say, Jesus was crucified by the ordinary sins of every day. We are all in this together. Our heart and conscience tell us, when we stand on Calvary, that what we see there is our own work, that the sins we so lightly condone result always in the crucifixion of the Son of God. In this sense, to quote a great Christian concept, the Lamb is 'slain from the foundation of the world' (Revelation 13:8), and still is slain today. 'Jesus,' said Pascal, 'will be in agony until the end of the world.'

O break, O break, hard heart of mine
    Thy weak self-love and guilty pride
His Pilate and his Judas were:
    Jesus, our Lord, is crucified!

So the cross of Jesus reveals the true nature and colour of sin, and by so doing creates saving penitence. This is one great secret of its power.

On the other hand, *it reveals God's almighty love*. Not to appease an angry God, not to induce him to change his mind and love us, did Jesus die; any such idea is definitely un-Christian. God's love is eternal and unchanging. There never was a time when God had to be persuaded to love. No, Calvary was not an inducement Jesus offered to God: it was God's own love in action. Just as from a volcano there flashes out now and then for one sudden, startling moment the elemental fire which burns unseen at the earth's heart, so, at the cross of Jesus, God's love leapt out in history, sheer flame, showing in that crowning moment of time what God is in his inmost being for ever. The cross reveals the heart of the eternal. It makes grace real. It makes love available for needy souls. It reconciles the sinful, and brings the world to God's feet.

XX
The Triumph

1 *The* DEFEAT *of* DEATH

LET us look at two pictures. One is an upper room in Jerusalem on the night after Calvary, and a little group of men cowering behind bolted and barricaded doors. Fear is on every face. But even more markedly than fear, dejection is written there, hopeless, final, irretrievable dejection. Dazed and stunned and bewildered they sit in silence, too heartbroken to speak, too benumbed in soul to pray. Everything is at an end. Fate has beaten them. There is nothing left to live for. That is the one picture – utter, abject defeat.

Here is the other. A few weeks later. The same group of men. But not skulking behind closed doors now! They are out in the streets. They are men aflame with superhuman confidence. Their words ring like iron. They have a message to which the world cannot but listen. They are absolutely fearless and overwhelmingly happy. They are planning the conquest of the earth.

Look first at the one picture and then the other – there the misery of blasted hopes, here the valour of the saints; there a fumbling, futile remnant, here the nucleus of a marching, militant Church – and only the briefest span of time between. How has this startling, almost incredible change in these men's lives occurred? Can we explain it? Yes. Between the two pictures something had happened – *Christ was risen*.

Never did an enterprise look more utterly ruined than when

Jesus of Nazareth was taken down from the cross and laid in the tomb. 'He was crucified, dead, and buried,' says our Apostles' Creed – the very words seem burdened with an awful finality. If the disciples thought about the future at all, they saw themselves creeping back shamefacedly to the homes they had once left so eagerly at Jesus' bidding, and they heard in fancy the jeers and taunts of the village street as they so ingloriously returned. 'I go a fishing,' said Simon Peter, but he knew all too well that even if he took up again the old life where he had laid it down, it could never content him now: his experience of Jesus had come in between, and that had spoilt him for anything else for ever. Not only was Christ dead: Christianity was dead. And against its tomb a great stone of despair had been rolled.

Yet it may have been that in one heart here and another there, some dim thought may have hovered that what they had witnessed at Calvary was not and could not be the end. In John Masefield's drama, *The Trial of Jesus*, there is a striking passage in which Longinus, the Roman centurion in command of the soldiers at the cross, comes back to Pilate to hand in his report on the day's work. The report is given; and then Procula, Pilate's wife, beckons to the centurion and begs him to tell her how the prisoner died. When the story has been told, 'Do you think he is dead?' she suddenly asks. 'No, lady,' answers Longinus, 'I don't.' 'Then where is he?' 'Let loose in the world, lady, where neither Roman nor Jew can stop his truth.' Standing in the shadow of the cross, where the cleanest, noblest soul who ever walked this earth hangs dying, we hear an inward voice telling us that this cannot be the end. It was not the end. In the great, simple words of the Creed, 'The third day he rose again from the dead; He ascended into heaven, and sitteth on the right hand of God the Father Almighty'.

2 *the* RESURRECTION: HISTORIC FACT

The evidence for the Resurrection is irrefutable. Divergences of detail may certainly be found in the various Gospel accounts of this supreme event. But these, far from shaking and destroying the credibility of the narratives, actually enhance it. Think of the circumstances. Here were the disciples, caught up in a whirl of stupendous amazement and bewilderment by the discovery that their Lord was still alive. Here were the other eye-witnesses of the event – Mary Magdalene and others – living through a time of supreme emotion and excitement. Is it any wondered that, when at a later day the Evangelists came to gather the memories of these crowded, glorious hours and to set them down in their Gospels, some differences of detail should have appeared? Does that detract in the smallest degree from the value of their evidence? On the contrary, we should have had far more reason to be uneasy if such differences had not been there. For then it would have been hard to resist the conclusion that the various accounts had been deliberately harmonised. A good illustration of the way in which such surface variations as we find here are bound to come into reports of stirring and exciting events, is provided by the experience of the Great War: eye-witnesses of one particular incident would describe it, each in his or her own way. The Gospel evidence for the Resurrection of Jesus bears the marks of reality and authenticity on the very face of it. It is the witness of those who were themselves utterly convinced, and from first to last it carries conviction.

It is a point of quite exceptional importance that when, just fifty days after the Crucifixion, the apostolic preaching of the Resurrection began in Jerusalem, *the evidence convinced thousands*. If the facts were not true, which the apostles were openly declaring, and declaring with such startling results, then obviously now – when the alleged occurrence itself was so recent – now was the time for their enemies to challenge the facts and disprove them. There were people in Jerusalem who wanted nothing better than to see the new movement nipped in the bud, and we may be sure that if by any means the central theme of the apostolic message could have been discredited and proved to be false, they would have lost no time in doing it. But no such refutation of the apostles' case was forthcoming. Easy as it would obviously at that time have been, if Jesus in fact had never risen from the dead, to prove that he had not risen – no such proof was even attempted. This failure on the part of Jesus' enemies is itself first-rate evidence of the truth of what the apostles were declaring. The facts remained unchallenged because they were above challenge. The Resurrection Gospel was incontestable.

But quite apart from documentary evidence, a clear witness lies in *the amazing transformation of the disciples themselves*, to which reference has already been made. It takes the Resurrection, nothing less, to explain the sudden and complete change in these men from absolute despair and futility to absolute radiance and mastery of life. This is the rock on which any theory of an invented story or of a mere visionary fancy goes to pieces. The idea that the disciples, having lost their Master, fabricated a tale of his return to them, is negated and made absurd by the lives of the men themselves. Inventions do not transform characters, men do not endure martyrdom for impostures. Every attempt which has been made to explain the disciples' belief on a purely visionary basis has ended by raising far more problems than it solved. One thing, one thing alone, makes what happened to these eleven men credible: Christ was risen indeed.

The evidence, however, goes beyond the original disciples – it includes *the fact of the Christian Church.* It is a simple fact of history that it was the resurrection belief that brought the Church into being; and when the Church swept out from Jerusalem to the conquest of the earth, it was the Resurrection message that was the driving-power. The truth of the amazing facts with which the closing chapters of our four Gospels deal, is witnessed to by the whole course of Christian history for nineteen centuries; for no one seriously believes that a spiritual movement like the Church, so indestructible in its nature, so limitless in its possibilities, so indispensable in its value for the souls of mankind, could ever have spring from, or been inspired by, anything which was not utterly and genuinely real. If Christ had not verily risen, the Church which bears his name would have perished long ago, for fierce attacks (social, political, intellectual) have been launched against it down the years. Many a time, indeed, it has seemed doomed and dead, and the grave-diggers – Hume, Voltaire and others – have been busy at its tomb; but always it has broken the grave, and rolled the stone away. Only the fact of the Resurrection of Jesus can explain the Church of the living God.

All these lines of evidence are valid and of great importance. But the supreme proof of the Resurrection, the thing which makes it not only credible but inevitable, is *the person of Jesus himself*. Now this is what the disciples, after the first startling shock had given place to steady certitude, came to see. Jesus being who and what Jesus was, anything other than that he should rise again was unthinkable. As one of themselves, on reflection, expressed it, 'It was not possible that he should be holden of death' (Acts 2:24). That was a great conviction, and our study of the life of Jesus with his disciples must have disclosed some of the factors that entered into it.

One thing which had always impressed these men about their Master was *his sheer vitality*. 'In him was life,' says John (John 1:4); 'the Prince of Life,' Peter calls him (Acts 3:15). Open your Gospels at any page, and the first thing which strikes you is that here is someone as radiant as the face of the morning, as vital as the breath of God. Everyone who came into contact with Jesus felt that he had enormous reserves at his command, and that however much they saw in him, there was always more behind. This explains the astounding daring of the requests they brought to him. Leprosy, for instance, was notoriously incurable; but 'Lord, if thou wilt,' said the leper simply, 'thou canst make me clean' (Matthew 8:2). They could not conceive any situation for which Christ would not be adequate. Even death would have to give way.

Moreover, there was *the love of Jesus*. From the first day his disciples had known him, that love had had the stamp of deathlessness upon it. It had flooded their whole world with a light which never was on sea or land. Such a love could never be robbed of its object. It would break the tomb, to stand beside its own.

But even more important was *the sinlessness, the moral perfection, of Jesus*. We have seen already, in our study of the healing miracles of Jesus, how intimately the Master's mighty works were bound up with, and dependent upon, the fact of his own sinlessness (see chapter XI, 'The Ministry of Healing'). In Jesus, alone amongst the sons of men, the final break with sin has been achieved; and the power of spirit over matter, which in others was blocked and thwarted at every turn by sin's taint and bias, was in him fully set free. Mighty works thus flowed naturally from Jesus, and the Resurrection, the mightiest of all, ceased to be impossible or even improbable, and became inevitable.

The decisive thing for these disciples was *their personal experience of Jesus*. Daily fellowship with him had taught them he was more than man; and though Calvary momentarily dimmed and clouded that high faith, it shone out clear again. Having come to feel towards Jesus as they had always felt towards God, they saw now that the Resurrection had been certain from the first: if Jesus died, and that were all, then God himself would die. So in the last resort, the proof of the Resurrection is the person of Jesus himself and men's experience of Jesus. It was not possible that he – God incarnate – should be holden of death.

3 *The* MASTER *reunited with his* FRIENDS

We turn now from the fact of the Resurrection to the recorded appearances of the Risen One. The first to see Jesus after his death was Mary Magdalene (John 20:1,11; cf Matthew 28:1,9). The greatest news that ever broke upon the world, the news which was to change the whole life of humanity and shake down thrones and revolutionise kingdoms, the news which still today girdles the earth with everlasting hope and sends a new thrill through every Christian soul on Easter morning, was given first to one humble, obscure woman out of whom seven devils had gone, who had nothing to distinguish her but her forgiven heart, and no claim at all but her love. Mary had come out, before dawn was in the sky, to sit beside a dead body. She was telling herself that everything else but that was gone – the voice of Jesus that would never speak again, the light in those eyes that would shine no more, the living soul that was fled for ever – all gone, and only the dead body left for love and gratitude to cling to and try to serve. She came, and even that was gone. This was her moment of final desolation. 'They have taken away my Lord, and I know not where they have laid him.' Blinded with tears, her eyes could not recognise someone standing near, but he called her by her name, and then she knew. 'Jesus saith unto her, Mary. She turned herself, and saith unto him, Rabboni; which is to say, Master.' What she had once been saved from and forgiven for was the measure of her devotion; and always it is those who love Jesus best, who see him first.

Luke records the beautiful story of the Christ of the Emmaus road (Luke 24:13ff). Of all possible disappointments in life, to be disappointed in Jesus Christ must surely be the worst: and that was the disappointment which was burdening the hearts of Cleopas and his friends as they journeyed home in the falling twilight. Brokenly they spoke to each other of the hope that was gone, and memories of happier days came crowding in –

days when, looking at Jesus, so young and strong and steady-eyed and godlike, they had been sure that this was the coming King and the Captain of ten thousand souls: 'We trusted that it had been he which should have redeemed Israel.' Now it had all ended in disillusionment, heartache and regret.

But Christ is often nearest when people think him gone for ever, and as they listened to the talk of the stranger who had joined them on the way, their hearts began to burn. Almost before they knew it, they had reached their journey's end: never surely had the Jerusalem to Emmaus road been so short as on that night. It was hard to say goodbye to the stranger whose company had so mysteriously charmed their gloom away and brought cheerfulness breaking in, and something guided them to keep him with them a little longer and to invite him to their table. There something happened: was it some familiar gesture as he broke the bread? Or was it in the grace he said over the simple meal? Or was it the hands in which he raised the bread, hands marked with nails? Whatever it was, it rent the veil which had been hanging before their eyes, and they knew him, and called him by his name.

That same night in Jerusalem the lost and leaderless disciples were reunited with their Master. 'When the doors were shut … came Jesus, and stood in the midst' (John 20:19; cf Luke 24:36). Two of the disciples were missing in that great hour – Judas and Thomas. Judas, in the restrained and solemn language of the Book of Acts, had gone 'to his own place' (Acts 1:25). But where was Thomas? Doubtless he was wandering alone in the dark, brooding on his own deep grief, and unable to bear any company now, not even the company of his fellow-disciples. He may even have been haunting the deserted slopes of Calvary. Next morning when Peter and John, with a strange new light on their faces, accosted him and shared with him their wonderful tidings, he looked at them sadly and told them they were deluded.

But a week later Thomas was in the upper room; and Jesus, who is always so patient with honest doubt, came again. This time the Master's self-revelation was specifically adapted to his one groping follower's need. Thomas now saw what the others had already seen, and entered into their experience; and with a great cry, 'My Lord and my God', he swept the midnight from his soul.

Reading the Evangelists' narratives of the appearances of the Risen Lord, we are struck by this notable fact: that while the Jesus whom these men and women saw was certainly the same dear Master whom they had known in bygone days, there was none the less a difference. There was a certain reserve about him now. 'Touch me not,' he said (John 20:17). It could not be called aloofness, but at least it meant that one chapter in the book of their fellowship together was now closed, and another chapter, a higher order of fellowship, beginning: Ordinary limitations of space and time had ceased to hold him: he came to them, and went in ways they could not understand (Luke 24:36; John 20:19). Recognition did not always happen immediately, as we have seen already in the stories of Mary in the garden and the Emmaus travellers. 'When they saw him, some doubted' (Matthew 28:17). 'He appeared in another form' (Mark 16:12). 'They supposed that they had seen a spirit' (Luke 24:37). 'Jesus stood on the shore: but the disciples knew not that it was Jesus' (John 21:4). He was the same – yet different. He was still the friend with whom in former days they had walked through the cornfields of Galilee and bivouacked at night beneath the open sky, the Master who had taught them such memorable lessons from the lilies of the field and the birds of the air, from yokes and ploughs and candlelight and the children shouting at their games. Yet somehow they were conscious of a change. But that, as they came to understand, was only to be expected. For he had been on a long journey since Calvary had snatched him from them. He had returned from the undiscovered country from whose bourne no traveller (it was thought) could ever return. And the breath of that other country was all about him. He belonged no longer to this narrow, material world, with its time and space restrictions: no, he belonged to that ampler, higher world of spirit which alone is real and eternal.

4 *The* INNER MEANING *of the* RESURRECTION

We have dwelt in this study upon the fact of the Resurrection, and upon those recorded appearances by which the fact was first heralded. We turn now finally to the inner meaning of the fact. It is obvious that an event like this must have had consequences, not only for the disciples, or even for the Church, but for the whole world. What did the Resurrection of Jesus mean?

It meant, first, God's vindication of his Son. When the disciples went out preaching and proclaiming their Risen Lord, they used significantly the passive, not active voice, to describe the event; they said regularly, not 'He rose,' but 'He was raised' – for with deep spiritual insight they saw that what had happened had been nothing less than God in action, God's right arm made bare on behalf of his beloved Son (Acts 2:24, 32; 3:15; 4:10; Romans 6:4, 9; I Corinthians 15:15). That one who had died a felon's death should be Messiah was an idea not only shocking, but actually blasphemous, to orthodox Jewish minds, and many devout people who had secret hopes about Jesus must have considered that the cross finished his pretensions. But here in the Resurrection was God's sudden, unexpected attestation of the very highest and most daring hopes that had ever been cherished about Jesus, God's own seal set convincingly to Jesus' Messianic claim, God's final vindication of his Son.

It meant, further, the vindication of righteousness. Daringly and gallantly Jesus had staked everything he had and was, upon the absolute validity of goodness and truth and love. These were the things whose supremacy he had always preached: for these he had consecrated his own life up to the last limit of self-consecration; and for his belief in these he was ready at last to die. Had the sinless Jesus remained in the tomb, the conclusion would have been irresistible that this world is a moral chaos, and goodness a poor mirage, and honour a mischievous delusion. But on the Resurrection morning it was just as if the whole nature of things by one mighty act had endorsed and countersigned the noble, unselfish way of living. We know now that the universe itself is on the side of the person who fights the good fight. Jesus rose: and righteousness was vindicated.

The Resurrection meant also the assurance of immortality. Pagans, watching Christ's people at work in the world, were struck by many things, but by nothing more forcibly than the Christians' contempt of death: and it was the Risen Christ who had robbed the king of terrors of his power. 'I go to prepare a place for you,' he had said, 'and I will come again and receive you unto myself' (John 14:2, 3); and if death meant that, what room was there for fear? The Master's conquest of death involved theirs. 'Because I live, ye shall live also' (John 14:19). Easter morning brought immorality to light; and the Christians, seeing death lying broken, could say with the Psalmist, 'God is gone up with a shout, the Lord with the sound of a trumpet' (Psalm 47:5).

Finally, the Resurrection meant a Christ alive for evermore. Even when the forty wonderful days succeeding the first Easter were over and Jesus' visible presence was withdrawn, the disciples knew they had not lost him. Every day his own word was being verified in their experience – 'Lo, I am with you always, even unto the end' (Matthew 28:20). Through all the vicissitudes of their active service, it was no fading memory that sustained them, but a living presence and a daily comradeship; and when, like their Master before them, they saw death coming to meet them violently, it was his hands that held them up. Nor was their experience unique. Hosts of men and women since the disciples' day have walked and talked with Christ. This is no miracle. If Christ is risen indeed, which means if he is living now, what is more natural than that his own friends should sometimes meet him face to face? Such fellowship is a direct consequence of the Resurrection. There was a day when Matthew Arnold, looking out upon the world, found himself crying ...

Oh, had I lived in that great day,
How had its glory new
Fill'd earth and heaven, and caught away
My ravish'd spirit too! ...
Now he is dead! Far hence he lies
In the lorn Syrian town;
And on his grave, with shining eyes,
The Syrian stars look down.

No. Arnold was wrong. He was utterly and finally wrong. Why seek the living among the dead? Christ is alive! Dr Dale, the great preacher of Birmingham, described how one day, while he was writing an Easter sermon, the fact of the Resurrection broke in upon him as it had never done before. '"Christ is alive." I said to myself: "alive!" and then I paused: – "alive!" and then I paused again: "alive! Can that really be true? living as really as I myself am?" I got up and walked about repeating, "Christ is living! Christ is living!" At first it seemed strange and hardly true, but at last it came upon me as a burst of sudden glory.'

Yes, Christ is alive. To thousands upon thousands at the present hour this is no mere theory or vague, uncertain rumour, but proved, inviolable experience; and if they are facing life victoriously now where once they were defeated, it is because they have found the same Risen Lord who walked among the flowers of the garden on the morning of the first Easter day.

XXI
Master and Lord of Life

1   CHRIST'S FINISHED *and* UNFINISHED WORK

WE have come now to the end of the story. But the end of the story of Christ is a beginning. The four Evangelists to whom we owe the story were fully conscious of this, and it never occurred to them to write *'finis'* when the last page was complete. As each of them laid down his pen and closed his book, he felt that what he had written was only volume one, the first instalment of a story which still was being enacted and was destined to continue through unborn generations and ages without number. One of them – Luke – at a later time took up his pen again to give the world volume two; and he prefaced this second instalment of the story of Christ – *The Acts of the Apostles,* he called it – with a reference to his original book: 'The former treatise have I made of all that Jesus *began* both to do and teach' (Acts 1:1); for Luke saw that however much of the story he had told, there was vastly more to follow. In a sense, of course, the task of Jesus on this earth was finished when he returned to his Father.

> '*All his work is ended,*'
>   *Joyfully we sing:*
> '*Jesus hath ascended!*
>   *Glory to our King!*'

'Christ, being raised from the dead,' said St Paul, 'Dieth no more' (Romans 6:9). All that was over. The earthly ministry, the agony of Gethsemane, the arrest and trial, the weariness of the Via Dolorosa, the death on the cross – all that was finished, and would never happen again. These were historic events. They came, and passed. They happened once, and only once. The full price of sin was paid. The revelation of redeeming love was perfect and complete. Nothing was left undone. Nothing remains to be added. Beyond Jesus we need never hope to go. In this sense, at any rate, it is true that the story of Jesus finds at Calvary and the empty tomb and the Ascension its culmination and completion and crown.

True – but not the whole truth. For while the Gospel is securely and solidly rooted in history, with its roots firmly twined round the unshakable rock of historic fact, the Christ of the Gospel is more than a mere figure of history. It was no historic reminiscence which got hold of Saul of Tarsus outside Damascus, and flung him violently to the ground from his horse, and revolutionised his life. It was no old, remembered story which sent the Christian message flaming like a prairie fire across the earth. It was something more than the recollection of a noble example which made men glow as the men of Pentecost glowed, sing as the Franciscans sang, and die as the Covenanters died. The fact of the matter is that the first volume of the life of Christ, the evangelic record, has been followed by a hundred others; and one is actually being written at the present hour wherever down the crowded streets of life the Master moves, seeking and finding the lost, binding up the broken-hearted, and driving out devils in the name of the Lord God Almighty. The story had not ended when Calvary and Easter were past. It had only just begun.

The first disciples realised this very clearly. Knowing Jesus as they now knew him, they could not conceive any lower place for him than the throne of the whole earth. Jesus, they saw, must be Master and Lord of life. So they dedicated themselves to the magnificent, amazing adventure which was to carry the cross in less than three hundred years from the ignominy of Golgotha to the throne of the Caesars. On the face of it, it seemed impossible that these few men, with no weapons to wield save one, the weapon of love, should make any impression on a world that had the weapon of force and was determined to use it. It seemed impossible that they should stand up against the vested interests of materialism and secularism, the 'principalities and powers' of which Paul spoke, and the entrenched selfishness of the world. When they first set out, with their unheard-of dream looking out of their eyes, the world simply laughed them to scorn. And when in spite of laughter and scorn they kept going on, marching indomitably from town to town and land to land until they were knocking at the gates of Rome, the world began to take them seriously and tried to bar their way. But by this time, blazing fire and torturing rack and furious insult were all in vain. The dream prevailed, and the world was at their feet. It was not their own achievement, they always said, but Christ's. It was the life-story, whose first volume contained Bethlehem and Galilee and Calvary, being continued. It was still Christ in action, and working in the earth.

And they were right. Nothing but the life of Christ in these men can explain the power they evidenced. On various levels that power made itself felt. It was power *on the physical level*. New and exhilarating energies were liberated in their very bodies, enabling them to carry through with zest and verve things which to other men would have been impossible. It was power *on the mental level*. Ill-educated and illiterate many of these early followers of Christ may have been; but something had happened to them which gave them a power of initiative, a grasp of essentials, and a directness of decision the like of which the world had never seen before. It was power *on the moral level.* Some of them had been rescued from devouring and devastating passions; some had to fight hot, stubborn temptations; some had to live in cities that were dens of corruption; and yet, spotless and white-robed and uncorrupted, they kept the narrow way, clean with the very cleanness of Jesus. It was power *on the spiritual level.* Wherever they went, other lives were changed and souls redeemed, and mighty miracles of grace were witnessed. Never for a moment did they dream of claiming for themselves the credit of all this power. Their explanation of it was at once incredibly simple and incredibly daring. It was Christ in them. It was a new Gospel being written. It was a new, wonderful stage in the story of their Master's life. And because of that, they knew that nothing could ever frustrate them or bring their adventure to defeat.

> *March we forth in the strength of God, with the banner of Christ unfurled,*
> *That the light of the glorious Gospel of truth may shine throughout the world:*
> *Fight we the fight with sorrow and sin, to set their captives free,*
> *That the earth may be filled with the glory of God, as the waters cover the sea.*

2 *The* PASSION *to make* CHRIST KING

Four things drove the early disciples out into the world to witness to Jesus as Lord and Master – four things which still, in the altered circumstances of today, lay the duty of witness upon every true disciple.

First, there was *the command of Jesus himself.* 'All power is given unto me in heaven and in earth. Go ye therefore, and teach all nations' (Matthew 28:18f). This world outlook has indeed characterised the life and teaching of Jesus from the first (eg Matthew 5:14; 8:11; 24:14; 26:13); but with this clear and definite command now ringing in their ears, the disciples could not doubt what their Lord required of them. St Luke records the fact that when Jesus gave his followers their commission, he added the words, 'beginning at Jerusalem' (Luke 24:47). That is an interesting touch, suggesting that a person's witness to Christ should start right on the very spot where he or she happens to be. Jerusalem had been the scene of the disciples' failure and shameful desertion of their Master in his hour of need; in the same place, they were now to give their witness and stand up for him before the eyes of all mankind. And was it not wonderfully in keeping with the love and patience and forgiving spirit which they had always seen in Jesus, that the city which had killed him should, by his own decree, be the first to receive their Gospel? But the message starting there, was to be carried across the world. This was their Lord's command; and they knew that on their obedience to it, their very fellowship with him would depend.

All Christian service in the world has that command behind it. Christ does not ask his friends as a favour to bear witness to him among men: he claims it as a duty. 'Ye are my friends, if ye do whatsoever I command you' (John 15:14). Christianity does not mean complimenting Christ as genius, or artist, or teacher: it means bowing to Christ as Commander. 'When ye shall have done all those things which are commanded you, say, We are unprofitable servants: we have done that which was our duty to do' (Luke 17:10). And when people say, as they sometimes do, that they can see no reason why the Church of Christ should go crusading at the ends of the earth while there is still so much to do at home and so many untaken forts in the rear of Christ's advance, the answer must be, not only that it is the very death of religion when it is not propagating itself and scattering itself abroad, but also that they are mistaken in imagining that this is in any sense an open question. It is emphatically *not* an open question. The great command settled it once for all. And the person who still debates and argues it is daring to correct Jesus Christ. That wrecks that person's position. The Master's ruling has been given; and he means it to be obeyed.

The second thing which sent the disciples out to witness in the world was *the urgency of the situation*. They were convinced that the end of the world was at hand. It might happen in their own lifetime. Had not Jesus assured them that some would not taste death till they had seen the Son of Man coming in his Kingdom (Matthew 16:28)? Were his own words not written on their hearts – 'Verily I say unto you that this generation shall not pass, till all these things be done' (Mark 13:30)? Clearly no time must be lost if the evangelisation of the world was to be achieved before the end came. 'The Gospel must first be published among all nations' (Mark 13:10). The King's business required haste, for the heedless world was perishing. Everywhere people were sitting in darkness and the shadow of death, hopeless and godless and lost and ruined: and the end was hurrying on. Christ's men were driven forth to preach by the sheer urgency of the situation.

This, too, lays the duty of witness upon their successors today. One startling factor in the present world situation is the breakdown among masses of people of ancient systems of belief and conduct, which has left them without guiding principles of any kind – like ships on stormy seas, without rudder or compass; and it is not speaking in any alarmist fashion to say that unless we can confront that situation with Christ, it may in the long run overwhelm us and lead the world back to chaos. This is a day when every one who has been with Jesus, and believes in Jesus, ought to feel himself called, by the very urgency of the situation, to be a living witness to Jesus in the world.

The third thing which drove the disciples out was *the glory of the message*. They had found something, the like of which had never burst upon the world before. There was the wonder of forgiveness, for instance. Other religions were, no doubt, ready to tell those who had sinned of a way by which, with hard, painful effort, they might creep slowly back to decency again; but Christ's religion spoke of God's arms around the most ragged and muddiest of souls. Or think of death, through fear of which mankind had always been subject to bondage; here were men who could laugh in death's grim face, for Christ had conquered. Moreover, God, in the thoughts of half the world, was a jealous, threatening, implacable tyrant: but Christ's men knew – and it thrilled their hearts with joy unspeakable to know it – that God was love and nothing but love, and love for evermore. They had found a reality beyond the world's furthest dreams, and it was the glory of the message that drove them forth and sent them flaming round the earth.

'They who have the torch,' says an old Greek proverb, 'must pass on the light'; and every disciple today who has once grasped the truth that the Gospel which he professes is far and away the most glorious thing which ever entered the heart of man, is bound to be a herald. As Temple Gairdner of Cairo put it, 'The true appeal for missions is that if Christ prayed those prayers (the prayers of Gethsemane and Calvary), then of course the world must know'. At the heart of the Christian message stands the magnificent, magnetic, adorable figure of Jesus Christ himself. The very glory of that message must constrain our witness.

The fourth thing which sent the disciples out (and this really included all the others) was the conviction which they embodied in the earliest Christian creed – *Jesus is Lord.* The very first Christian sermon which was ever preached culminated with the words, 'God hath made that same Jesus, whom ye have crucified, both Lord and Christ' (Acts 2:36); and it was this Lordship of Jesus that was the heart of everything. In Paul's statement, 'We preach Christ Jesus as Lord' (II Corinthians 4:5), the theme of all the early preaching is summarised; and the simple confession 'Jesus is Lord' was the sole creed of the earliest days (Romans 10:9; I Corinthians 12:3; Acts 10:36). Nineteen centuries of Christianity have made this title familiar, and perhaps have dulled its wonder for us. But when the first disciples, borrowing from their Old Testament the very word which the Greek version had used to translate the Hebrew 'Jehovah', took this name and applied it to the Master with whom they had walked the roads of Galilee, it was a mighty achievement of faith. By this title they meant that the friend to whom they owed so much was one day to be Judge of all mankind. The voice whose every accent they knew and loved would yet awaken the whole earth like a trumpet. All the kingdoms of the world would be his, and he would be Lord indeed. Despised and rejected of men these disciples often might be, as their Master had been before them; but through it all, they kept dreaming their dreams, envisaging for their Leader an empire greater than anything that every swam into Caesar's ken, and planning for him a world strategy compared with which all the campaigns of an Alexander were a mere nothing. When groups of them met together in that hostile, contemptuous world, 'He is Lord of all,' they whispered; and their password was 'Maranatha' – 'Lord, come!' (I Corinthians 16:22; cf Revelation 22:20).

Far simpler than any subsequent confession of faith which people have arrived at, the creed 'Jesus is Lord' is nevertheless profound in its meaning and world-shaking in its consequences. To apply it faithfully involves asserting the absolute sovereignty of Jesus over every department of one's own life first, and then over all the life of the world. It means the throne of the universe for Christ. It is still a daring claim, as it was at the first; but no one who has honestly faced the fact of Christ can have any doubt at all that that throne is his by right. It has been bought with a price – bought with the hunger in the desert when he would not make the stones into bread; bought with the tears he shed over the sins of men; bought with the sweat at Gethsemane which was like great drops of blood; bought with the bitter cross where they broke his body in death; bought with the deathless love which through all the years has refused resolutely to let a lost world go. The Captain of the hosts of humanity has himself been in the ranks. He has experienced the hardship and peril of life's campaign from the common soldier's side. He has endured the discipline. If he rides at the head of the host today, it is because he once marched on foot. If one day he is to be King over all the sons of men, it is because at the first he was not ashamed to call us brethren. 'Wherefore,' says Paul finely, summing up in that word the whole story of Jesus' sufferings and sorrows, 'wherefore God also hath highly exalted him, and given him a name which is above every name, that at the name of Jesus every knee should bow' (Philippians 2:9).

Yes, Christ's sovereign rights have been bought with a price. This is he who came out of great tribulation: therefore it is he upon the throne. And our own conscience bears witness that this is his due place. Like the centurion of Capernaum (Matthew 8:9) who felt instinctively that Jesus had 'soldiers under him', unseen powers to do his bidding, and that behind him was all the weight and majesty of empire, so we feel and know, with everything that is deepest and truest within us, that his Kingdom cannot fail, and that one day the whole universe of earth and heaven shall acknowledge him alone.

3 JESUS *shall reign*

That day has not yet dawned, but slowly and steadily it is coming nearer. Already one Figure can be seen standing where the roads of life meet. *Jesus is standing where the roads of nationality meet.* High up amongst the Andes Mountains, where the lands of Chile and the Argentine touch, there stands a great bronze statue of Christ, forged out of the metal of discarded guns; and on the base of the statue the words are engraved: 'Sooner shall these mountains crumble into dust than Argentines and Chileans break the peace they have sworn to maintain at the feet of Christ the Redeemer.'

Jesus is standing where the roads of class meet. General Booth of the Salvation Army used to insist that no man's arms were long enough to reach out and give a hand to rich and poor at once: human arms may not do it, but the arms which were stretched wide on Calvary can. *Jesus is standing where the roads of literature meet*. The world's literature for nineteen hundred years has been haunted by Jesus, haunted by his bleeding hands and feet, and by his burning eyes. Those two giants of British and American literature, Carlyle and Emerson, once met at Carlyle's Scottish home; and as they walked together over the hill, discussing all things in heaven and earth, the little village church came into view beneath them, and Carlyle stopped. Turning to Emerson he said, 'Christ died on the tree, that built Dunscore Kirk yonder; that brought you and me together. Time has only a relative existence'.

Jesus is standing where the roads of religion meet. Just before the World Missionary Conference in Jerusalem in 1928, an exhaustive and comprehensive survey was carried through of all the great non-Christian faiths. What was the result? In the words of Dr John Mott: 'It was overwhelmingly proved that the more open-minded, honest, just, and generous we were in dealing with the non-Christian faiths, the higher Christ loomed in his absolute uniqueness, sufficiency, supremacy and universality.' 'There is no one else,' said a prominent Hindu to Stanley Jones, 'who is seriously bidding for the heart of the world except Jesus Christ. There is no one else on the field.' Already one Figure is standing where the roads of all the ages meet; and to those who have once seen him, and experienced in their own lives his power, this above all else is certain: that a day is drawing near when every gate in the universe will be lifting up its head to let the King come in.

All this is true; and because it is true, one question leaps out on us from every page of the story of Jesus, one challenge which no soul can finally avoid: Is he Master and Lord of *my* life? Every year, many people enter the Church by profession of faith. That is to say, every year they stand up in public and take upon themselves a vow that they are going to make Christ Lord of all. Think what would happen if that multitude were witnessing for Christ with all their might! Think what would happen if our own lives were really his, with no 'ifs' and 'buts' and conditions and reservations, but his up to the very hilt. Think what it would mean for ourselves. Think what it would mean for the world around us. And think what it would mean for Christ.

> *O that, with yonder sacred throng,*
> *We at his feet may fall,*
> *Join in the everlasting song,*
> *And crown him Lord of all!*

Book References

Quotations from the Bible throughout this book are taken from:

The Authorised (or King James) Version of the Bible.

Other books used by the author and referred to in the original text:

Axling, William: *Kagawa.*
Craig, Milligan and Baillie: *Christian Faith and Practice.*
Matthews, Basil: *The Clash of World Forces.*
Smith, Edwin W: *Aggrey of Africa.*
Welch: *The Preparation for Christ in the Old Testament,* lessons III and XIX.